Society for the Preservation of the Irish Language

An Dara Leabhar Gaedhilge Second Irish book

Society for the Preservation of the Irish Language

An Dara Leabhar Gaedhilge Second Irish book

ISBN/EAN: 9783744735490

Printed in Europe, USA, Canada, Australia, Japan

Cover: Foto ©Andreas Hilbeck / pixelio.de

More available books at **www.hansebooks.com**

an Dara Leabar Gaedilge.

SECOND IRISH BOOK.

PUBLISHED FOR THE

Society for the Preservation of the Irish Language.

;

TENTH EDITION.

Twenty second and Twenty-third Thousand

DUBLIN:

M. H. GILL & SON

1890.

SOCIETY
FOR THE
Preservation of the Irish Language.

OFFICERS AND COUNCIL ELECTED, ST. PATRICK'S DAY, 1889, FOR YEAR, 1889-90.

Patron.
(*Permanent*).
HIS GRACE THE MOST REV. T. W. CROKE, D.D.
Archbishop of Cashel.

President.
RIGHT HON THE O'CONOR DON, P.C., D.L., M.R.I.A.

Vice-Presidents.
REV. SAMUEL HAUGHTON, M.D., D.C.L., F.R.S., S.F. T.C.D., President, Royal Irish Academy.
THE MOST REV. JOHN MACCARTHY, D.D., Bishop of Cloyne.
MARSHAL MACMAHON, Ex-Pres. of the French Republic.
THE MOST REV. PIERSE POWER, D.D., Bishop of Waterford and Lismore.

Hon. Treasurers.
REV. M. H. CLOSE, M.A., M.R.I.A.
COUNT PLUNKETT, B.L., M.R.I.A.

Hon. Secretaries.
RICHARD J. O'DUFFY.
BRIAN O'LOONEY, M.R.I.A., F.R.H.S.

Secretary of Council.
J. J. MACSWEENEY, R.I.A.

DUBLIN
6 MOLESWORTH STREET
1889.

MEMBERS OF COUNCIL.

Ali, Professor Mir Aulad, T.C.D.

Barry, Rev. Edmund, M.R.I.A., P.P., Rathcormac.

Bell, Hamilton, Esq., M.R.I.A., F.R.G.S.I.

Blackie, Professor, Edinburgh.

Close, Rev. M. H., M.A., Treasurer, Royal Irish Academy.

Conway, T. W., Esq., the Model Schools, Marlborough Street.

Corbet, W. J., Esq., M.P.

Cox, Michael F., Esq., M.D., M.R.I.A.

D'Arbois de Jubainville, Mons., Professor of Celtic in the College de France, Paris.

Dawson, Charles, Esq., T.C.

Dixon, Henry, Esq., Dublin.

Doherty, W. J., Esq., C.E., M.R.I.A.

Ernault, Mons. Emile, Poitiers.

Fitzgerald, Thomas, Esq., Ringsend.

Fitzgerald, The Most Rev. Wm , D.D., Bishop of Ross.

Goodman, Rev. James, M.A., T.C.D.

Halligan, James, Esq., Dublin.

Hart, C. H., Esq., A.B., Dublin.

Hennessy, Sir John Pope, K.C.M.G.

Holland, John, Esq., Ballinspital, Kinsale.

Lehane, D., Esq., Inspector of National Schools.

Lloyd, J. H., Esq., Dublin.

Lynch, Daniel, Esq., Dunleer.

MacCarthy, Rev. Professor Bartholomew, D.D., Todd Professor, Royal Irish Academy.

MacCarthy, Justin Huntly, Esq., M.P.

MacEnerney, Rev. F., C.C.

MacEniry, Major R., R.I.A.

MacSweaney, J. J., Esq., R.I.A.

MacSwiney, Rev. James, S.J.

MacTernan, Rev. S., P.P., M.R I.A, Killasnett.

Moloney, M., Esq., Inspector, National Schools.

Murray, Æneas J., Esq., Head Master of the Model Schools, Cork.

Nettlau, Dr. Max, Vienna.

Nolan, Pierce L., Esq., B.A., Dublin.

O'Byrne, E., Esq., Tarn, France.

O'Byrne, Rev. L., C.C., Bray.

O'Byrne, Paul, Esq., Dublin.

O'Donel, C. J., Esq., J.P. M.R.I.A.

O'Duffy, R. J., Esq., Dublin.

O'Hanlon, Very Rev. John, Canon, P.P., M.R.I.A.

O'Hart, John, Esq., M.H.S.

O'Looney, Brian, Esq., M.R.I.A.

O'Meagher, J. C., Esq., M.R.I.A.

O'Reilly, Prof. J. P., M.R.I.A.

O'Riordan, T., Esq., Ringsend.

Plunkett, Count, B.L., M.R.I.A.

Rhys, Professor, Oxford University.

Rooney, Thomas, Esq., Dublin.

Ryan, L. J., Esq., Head Master Marlboro' Street Model Schools

Ryding, Dr. F., Merrion Square.

Schuchardt, Professor, University of Gratz, Styria.

Sexton, Right Hon. Thomas M.P., Lord Mayor.

Sigerson, George, Esq., M.D., M.R.I.A.

Sladen, Rev. R., P.P., Modeligo.

Sullivan, T. D., Esq., M.P., T.C.

Swan, Rev. Brother, Superior of Christian Schools, North Richmond Street, Dublin.

Ward, T., Esq., Dublin.

Zimmer, Dr. H., Greifswald, Prussia.

With power to add

INTRODUCTION.

OF ASPIRATION AND ECLIPSIS.

THE learner will be now required to master Aspiration and Eclipsis. They are the first difficulties that the student will meet in learning the Irish language, and until he understands them he can make but little progress. Aspiration and eclipsis are peculiar to the Celtic languages, but they are fully carried out only in the Irish. Aspiration in Scotch Gaelic is nearly the same as in Irish, but in all the modern books printed in the Scotch dialect of our language, eclipsis *proper** is wanting. This omission seems unaccountable, for not only was the system of Eclipsis strictly observed in all books and manuscripts of Scotch Gaelic up to the beginning of the last century, but traces of it exist even yet in the spoken dialect of the Highlands. It is unfortunate that modern Scotch Gaelic scholars have adopted this change, thus depriving their mother tongue of an innate and peculiar beauty.

Aspiration and Eclipsis, although different grammatical peculiarities, agree in this that they have the effect of making ease of utterance consistent with grammatical precision.

Dr. O'Donovan remarks that a tendency to aspiration seems to be a conspicuous characteristic of all the dialects of the Celtic, and belongs to the Irish in particular. After giving many instances of words cognate with the Latin which are aspirated in Irish, he says : " Many of the same words, and others besides, are also aspirated in several of

* Eclipsis occurs in modern Scotch Gaelic only in the case of ſ eclipsed by c, as in such phrases as *chum an t-saoghail*, t the word ; *mún t-solus*, about the light.

the modern languages of Europe : as the French *moyen*
from *medium* (Irish meaʊon) ; *avoir*, from *habere* ; *mere*,
from *mater* (Irish, máċaıɲ), &c. In Italian—*avere*, from
habere ; *tavola*, from *tabula*, &c.

Even in English there is an occasional attempt at a softening of the sound, as, for instance, in such words as *thought*,
fraught, &c., where the letter *g* is aspirated, and the sound
made softer ; but in no language has the system of softening
the sounds of the consonants been brought to greater per-
fection than in Irish. It is well worth the labour incurred
to study the Irish Language, merely to understand the
beauty of Aspiration and Eclipsis, where two things totally
different and, in other languages, sometimes incompatible,
namely, euphony and grammatical precision, have been
brought together and so employed that the result achieved
is at once philosophic and beautiful.

The mark for Aspiration used in most modern Irish
printed books is a dot (·) placed over the consonant that
suffers a change from its original radical sound, as in the
word moċ, *early*, in which the c is aspirated, and gets the
sound of *ch* or *gh*. Instead of the dot over the aspirated
letter some writers prefer employing the letter h after it,
and write maıċ, *good*, thus, maıch. But using an h instead
of a dot has been objected to by our best Irish scholars, on
the ground that it makes the words unnecessarily long. For
instance, in writing the phrase, a ʊeaɲḃɲáıċɲeaċa, *his
brothers*, with the dot, only fifteen letters are employed ; but
if the h be used instead of the dot, thus, a ʊheaɲbhɲaıch-
ɲeacha, the phrase will contain nineteen letters. The dot
is therefore much the shorter and neater method of indicat
ing aspiration.

It is here necessary to remark that the term "aspiration,"
as generally used for denoting the change of sound referred
to, has not quite the same meaning in Irish as in English
Grammar ; because aspiration, as understood in English,
means the sound of the letter *h*, whereas all dotted consonants
in Irish do not take the sound of *h*, some taking the sound
of the English *y*, and some of *v*, and some of *w*. In some
instances the sound of the dotted letter is entirely suppressed.

SECOND IRISH BOOK

PART I.

ASPIRATION.

"Aspiration" is derived from *ad-spirare*, ꝺo breathe-to. It denotes the action of the breath, by which the primary sounds of certain consonants are changed into softer related sounds. Nine of the consonants are capable of this change, viz., b c ꝺ ꝼ ᵹ m p ꞃ ꞇ, of these all but ꝼ m and ꞃ are *stops* of the breath, that is to say, at the end of a syllable they cause a sudden stop to the emission of the breath, or they begin a syllable with a sudden explosion thereof. But when these consonants are aspirated or breathed-to, they retain no longer their abrupt pronunciation. For instance b, as in bᴀꝺ, is pronounced abruptly; but when this letter is aspirated or breathed-to, as it is in ḃᴀꝺ, its sound becomes like that of English *w*. ꝼ m and ꞃ, though already spirants, or pronounced with an emission of the breath, are nevertheless capable of a further aspiration so as to acquire their own secondary still softer sounds. It is necessary to distinguish between aspiration of a consonant as thus described and that of a vowel. Aspiration softens a consonant, but any additional breathing-to a vowel makes it stronger and rougher.

SECTION I.

SOUNDS OF THE ASPIRATED LETTERS.

In this section the sounds of the mutab'e letters when aspirated will be explained, and an Exercise given on each in which the letters so affected will be shown chiefly in radic il words, where they, to some extent, serve to express sounds that have no special symbo s in the Irish Alphabet. In the second Section the change of sound of these letters when influenced by certain parts of spee h shall be treated of.

Primary Form of the Mutable Letters.

ɓ. c. ᴐ. ꝼ. ᵹ. m. p. s. ᴅ.

Secondary (Aspirated) Form.

ɓ ċ ᴐ̇ ꝼ̇ ᵹ̇ ṁ ṗ ṡ ᴅ̇

ɓ ċ ᴐ̇ ꝼ̇ ᵹ̇ ṁ ṗ ṙ ċ

An approximation to the sound given at the head of each Exercise. ʟ, n, and ꝛ do not admit of aspiration. Aspirated as well as unaspirated consonants generally have a broad or slender sound according as the v wel which precedes or follows them is broad or slender ᴀ, o, u, are *broad,* e and ı, *slender* vowels.

EXERCISE I. ɓ.

ɓ *broad* sounds nearly like *w* in wool, as bu꜓ (*woor*), your. Between two *short broaa* vowels it is sounded softly, much like *w* in power, as ᵹᴀbᴀꝛ (*gower*), a goat

If the *broad* vowel preceding or following ḃ be *long*, it gets the sound either of *w* or *v*. ʼn Munster *v* is more generally heard.

Ḃ *slender* sounds exactly like *v*, as ḃí (*vee*), was.   When *final,* ḃ is usually sounded like *v,* as ʒaɾḃ, rough, pronounced *gorv.*

aʒaıḃ, at (or with) you.	ʒaɾḃ,[1] rough.
ḃí, was, were.	leaḃaɾ, a book.
ḃuɾ, your.	leanḃ,[1] a child.
ᴐuḃ, black.	lıḃ, with you.
ɾıoɾ-ḃuan, steadfast.	ɾḃ, you, ye.
ʒaḃaɾ, a goat.	ᴄaɾḃ,[1] a bull.
an, the.	ɾıoɾ, true.
buan, lasting.	ɾé, he, it.
caɾa, caɾaᴐ, } a friend.	ᴄá, is, are.

1. An ʒaḃaɾ. 2. ᴄaɾḃ ᴐuḃ. 3. Ḃı ɾḃ ʒaɾḃ. 4. Ḃı ɾé ᴐuḃ. 5. Ḃı an ʒaḃaɾ ᴐuḃ. 6. Ḃı leaḃaɾ aʒaıḃ. 7. ᴄá an leaḃaɾ aʒaıḃ. 8. Ḃuɾ leanḃ. 9. Caɾa ɾıoɾ-ḃuan. 10. Ḃı ʒaḃaɾ aʒaıḃ.

----

1. The goat. 2. A black bull. 3. Ye were rough. 4. He was black. 5. The goat was black. 6. A book was at you (you had a book.)[2] 7. The book is at you (you have the book.)[2] 8. Your child. 9. A steadfast friend. 10. A goat was at you (you had a goat).[2]

[1] For observations on " consonants combined," as nḃ and ɾḃ above, see *First Book*, page 19.

[2] For explanation of these idioms see observations on Exercises XIV. and XV. *First Irish Book.*

Obs.—The initial letter of the second part of a compound word (if it be aspirable), suffers aspiration for the sake of euphony, as in the example above—ꝼíoꞃ-ḃuᴀn (pronounced *feervooan*); ꝼíoꞃ, *true*, and ḃuᴀn, *lasting*, where the b is aspirated, to enable the two words to be more easily united. The sounds of the aspirable letters, when initial, are shown in these Exercises by words of this class, for aspirated letters do not *begin* radical words. The rule regarding formation of compound terms will not be entered into here.

Sıḃ, *you*, or *ye*, and ḃuꞃ, *your*, the second person *plural*, are never used for ᴄú, *thou*, and ᴅo, *thy*, the second person *singular*. A few *prepositional pronouns* are here introduced in which aspirated letters occur.

EXERCISE II. Ċ.

Ċ *broad* has always a deep guttural sound. The word loċ, *lough*, as generally pronounced in Ireland, will afford an example.

Ċ *slender* has a smooth guttural sound, as in cꞃíċ, a country, pronounced nearly like *creegh*.

Ċ *slender* when *final* is pronounced very faintly, as in ᴅeıċ, ten. These sounds are best learned by ear, as they do not now exist in English. Sometimes the slender sound of ċ is almost exactly *h*.

ᴀċᴛ, but.	eᴀċ, a steed.
ᴀmᴀċ, out.	ꝼᴀċ, a raven.
ᴀꞃᴛeᴀċ, in.	ꝼıċe, twenty.
cᴀoċ, blind.	ꝼíoꞃ-ċᴀꞃᴀ, a true friend
cloċ, a stone.	Lᴀoċ, a hero.
cloċᴀıꞃe, a stone-cutter	loċ, a lough, lake.
ċu� 5 ᴀm, to me, unto me.	luċ, a mouse.
ᴅeıċ, ten.	

ᴀᵹᴀm, at (or with me).   é, he, it.
ᴀᵹuꞃ, and.   iꞃ, is.
beiꞃ, bring, take.   ní, not.
cuiꞃ, put.

   1. Lᴀoċ ᴀᵹuꞃ eᴀċ.   2. Oeiċ ᴀᵹuꞃ ꞃíċe.
3. Cá ᴀn ꞃiᴀċ oub.   4. ní eᴀċ é ᴀċc ꞃiᴀċ.
5. Cá ᴀn loċ oub.   6. Oí ᴀn luċ cᴀoċ.
᾽. Cuiꞃ ᴀn luċ ᴀmᴀċ.   8. beiꞃ cloċ ᴀꞃceᴀċ
ċuᵹᴀm.   9. iꞃ cloċᴀiꞃe é.   10. Cá ꞃíoꞃ-ċᴀꞃᴀ
ᴀᵹᴀm.

---

   1. A warrior and a steed.   2. Ten and
twenty.   3. The raven is black.   4. Not a
steed it (it is not a steed)[1] but a raven.   5.
The lake is black.   6. The mouse was blind.
7. Put the mouse out.   8. Bring in a stone to
me.   9. He is a stone-cutter.[1]   10. A true
friend is with me (I have a true friend).

OBS.—ꞃíoꞃ-ċᴀꞃᴀ is a compound word; ꞃíoꞃ, *true*, and
cᴀꞃᴀ, *a friend*. See observations on preceding Exercise.
There are some adjectives which occasionally come before
the noun (and a few which always occur before it), and which
are exceptions to the general rule (see observations, Exercise
I., *First Book*); these usually form with the noun a compound word *as in the present example.*
  The learner will refer to Exercise XIV., *First Book*, for an
explanation of prepositions joined to pronouns.   In this and
the preceding Exercise we have Lib, from Le and ꞃib; ᴀᵹᴀib,
from ᴀᵹ and ꞃib; ċuᵹᴀm, from ċum and me; oꞃꞃᴀib, from
ᴀiꞃ and ꞃib.   ċuᵹᴀm is written and pronounced ċúᵹᴀm in
Munster.

   * See observations on Exercises III. and IV. *First Book.*

EXERCISE III. ȯ.

ȯ *broad* sounds somewhat like *gh* soft, or *y* broad and guttural, as ꞃᴀoꞃ-ȯuıne (ꞃᴀoꞃ, free, ȯuıne, a person), a freeman, pronounced nearly *saerghuine*.

ȯ *slender* sounds exactly like *y* in *y*ear, as ꝟıoꞃ-ȯılıꞃ (ꝟıoꞃ, *true,* ȯılıꞃ, *fond*), *sincere,* pronounced *feer-yeelish.*

ȯ *final* is *silent.*

ȯ in the body of a word (not a compound, is *silent.*

ȯ in such words as buıȯe (*bwee*) and cꞃoıȯe *(cree),* merely lengthens the sound of the preceding letters, and preserves the correct orthography, somewhat like *ʄh* in mi*gh*ty, thou*gh*, &c., in English.

ȯ in the first syllable of a word, if preceded by ᴀ or o, sounds like *i* in v*ie*, or *ey* in *eye*, as ᴀȯᴀꞃc *(eyark),* a horn. The exceptions to this rule are marked with an accent thus, ᴀȯ, *luck* (pronounced *aw*).

ᴀȯ, luck.
ᴀȯᴀꞃc, a horn.
ᴀȯmuȯ, timber.
buıȯe, yellow.
cꞃoıȯe, a heart.
ꝟıᴀȯ, a deer.
ꞡᴀeȯılıꞡ, } Irish
ꞡᴀcȯılꞡe, } Gaelic.

ꞡꞃᴀȯ, love.
mᴀȯᴀȯ, } a dog.
mᴀȯꞃᴀȯ, }
ꞃᴀȯᴀꞃc, sight.
ꞃuᴀȯ, red.
ꞃᴀoꞃ-ȯuıne, a freeman.

beo, living, alive.
ouine, a person.
ʒeup, sharp.
i, she, her, it.

oppaɩḃ, on you.
ʀaop, free, cheap.
ʀo, this.
ᴄpeun, brave.

1. Fɩaó aʒuʀ aóapc. 2. Maoaó puaó aʒuʀ eaċ buíóe. 3. Fɩaċ ouḃ aʒuʀ fɩaó buíóe. 4. Aómuo buíóe. 5. Aó aʒuʀ ʒʀáó. 6. Cá an fɩaó beo. 7. Iʀ leaḃaʀ ʒaeóɩlʒe é ʀo. 8. Cá paóapc ʒeup aʒaɩḃ. 9. Ḃi aó oppaɩḃ. 10. Cá cpoíóe cpeun aʒ ʀaop-ouine.

---

1. A deer and a horn. 2. A red dog and a yellow steed. 3. A (black) raven and a yellow deer. 4. Yellow timber. 5. Luck and love. 6. The deer is alive. 7. This is a Gaelic book. 8. (There) is sharp sight with you (ye have sharp sight). 9. Luck was on you (ye had luck). 10. (There) is a brave heart with a freeman (a freeman has a brave heart).

Obs.—The examples buíóe, &c., given above, afford instances of the diphthongs oí and uí (with accent on í) which are very seldom used.

Aómuo is pronounced in Munster without the accent.

So is never employed after the noun without the article being employed before the noun. See note 2, page 10, *First Book*.

EXERCISE IV. Ḟ.

Ḟ is not sounded, but the vowel following it is very forcibly pronounced. Ḟ is never *final*, and never occurs in the middle of words except compounds.

caoip-ḟeoil (sheep-flesh), mutton.

'ʒeapp-ḟiaḋ (*garrea*), a hare.

maipc-ḟeoil (beef-flesh), beef.

aʒ, at, or with.

ɼaopa, a sheep.

ɼeap, a man.

ɼeoil, flesh, meat.

muic-ḟeoil (swine flesh) pork.

ɼean-ḟeap (*shanar*), an old man.

cpeun-ḟeap, a brave man.

mapc, a beef.

muc, a pig.

ɼean, old.

1. Ḟiaḋ aʒuɼ ʒeapp-ḟiaḋ. 2. Sean-ḟeap aʒuɼ cpeun-ḟeap. 3. Caopa ɔuḃ aʒuɼ ʒeapp-ḟiaḋ puaḋ. 4. Caopa aʒuɼ caoip-ḟeoil. 5. Muc aʒuɼ muic-ḟeoil. 6. Mapc aʒuɼ maipc-ḟeoil. 7. Ʒaḃap buiḋe aʒuɼ ʒeapp-ḟiaḋ. 8. Ḃi ʒeapp-ḟiaḋ aʒ an ɼean-ḟeap. 9. Luċ aʒuɼ ʒeapp-ḟiaḋ. 10. Maipc-ḟeoil aʒuɼ muic-ḟeoil.

---

1. A deer and a hare. 2. An old man and a brave man. 3. A black sheep and a red hare. 4. A sheep and mutton. 5. A pig and pork. 6. A beef and beef. 7. A yellow goat and a hare. 8. A hare was with the old man (the old man had a hare). 9. A mouse and a hare. 10. Beef and pork.

EXERCISE V. Ʒ.

Ʒ *broad* and *slender,* sounds exactly like ḋ.

In the middle and end of words ġ is quiescent, but lengthens the preceding vowel.

Aġ, see rule for aḋ.

aġaiḋ (*eyee*), a face.
amuiġ, outside.
astiġ, inside.
deaġ (*dha*), good.
fóġluim, learn.

foiġid, } patience.
foiġide, }
laoġ, a calf.
ríġ, a king.
sóġ, pleasure.
tír-ġráḋ, patriotism.

aca, with them. sí, she. tír, land, country.

1. Ḃí an laoġ buíḋe. 2. Tá sé astiġ. 3. Ḃí sí amuiġ. 4. Aġaiḋ agus croiḋe. 5. Tá deaġ-ríġ aca. 6. Tá tír-ġráḋ agaiḃ. 7. Fóġluim Gaeḋilge. 8. Tír-ġráḋ agus foiġid. 9. Ḃí áḋ agus sóġ orraiḃ. 10. Amuiġ agus astiġ.

---

1. The calf was yellow. 2. He is inside. 3. She was outside. 4. Face and heart. 5. A good king is to them (they have, &c.). 6. Patriotism is to you (you have, &c.). 7. Learn Irish. 8. Patriotism and patience. 9. Luck and pleasure were on you. 10. Outside and inside.

OBS.—Amaċ and asteaċ (see exercise on ċ) are used when motion to or from a place is implied; amuiġ and astiġ when the object is stationary either inside or outside.

In words like ríġ, the final aspirated letter serves merely to preserve a fixed spelling, like *gh* in hi*gh* or in althou*gh*.

EXERCISE VI. ṁ.

ṁ *broad*, in the beginning of a word, is pro-nounced in the South like *v*, in the North and West like *w*. In the middle of words it is sounded very nasal.

ṁ *slender* always sounds like *v*. Wheᴸ *final*, ṁ broad or slender is usually soundeᴅ like *v*. The only difference between the sounds of ḃ and ṁ (*both dotted*) is that ṁ is generally nasal.

aṁáin (*avawin*), only.	ꝼollaṁ, empty.
anaṁ, seldom.	láṁ, a hand.
áꝑo-ṁeaꞃ, high regard.	naoṁ, a saint.
ꝺaṁ, an ox.	ꞃeaꞃṁaċ, firm.
ꝼeaꝑaṁail (*farooil*), manly.	ꞃeunṁaꝑ, prosperouꞃ
	talaṁ, earth.
aꝑ, on, on him.	meaꞃ, regard.
an, whether,	no, or, nor.
aon, one.	tiꝑm, dry.
áꝑo, high.	

1. Láṁ Láꝺoiꝑ. 2. Aon láṁ aṁáin. 3. ḃi an láṁ ꝼollaṁ. 4. Iꞃ anaṁ tá ꞃé ꝼollaṁ. 5. An ꝺaṁ aguꞃ an taꝑḃ. 6. ḃi áꝑo-ṁeaꞃ aꝑ an naoṁ. 7. An ꝼollaṁ no lán é? 8. An talaṁ tiꝑm. 9. Iꞃ ꞃeunṁaꝑ an ꝺuine é. 10. Iꞃ ꞃeaꞃṁaċ aguꞃ iꞃ ꝼeaꝑaṁail an caꝑa é.

---

1. A strong hand. 2. One hand only. 3. The hand was empty. 4. (It) is seldom it is empty. 5. The ox and the bull. 6. (There)

was high regard on the saint. 7. Whether empty or full it (is it empty or full)? 8. The dry earth. 9. It is prosperous the man he (he is a prosperous man). 10. He is a firm and manly friend.

OBS.—ᴀṁᴀɪl and ṁᴀp are suffixes, like *al* in English, by which adjectives are formed from nouns.

EXERCISE VII. ṗ.

ṗ is exactly like *ph* or *f*.

ceuᴅ-ṗpoinn (*kadhe-frinn*), breakfast (first meal).

móp-ṗiᴀn, great pain.

ull-ṗéipc, a monster (ull, great, and péipc), a great serpent.

ᴸonᴣ-ṗopc, a camp (lonᴣ, a ship, hence a tent, because resembling a ship in form, and popc).

ᴀnn, in it, therein.
ᴀnn pin, there, in that.
ᴀnn po, here, in this.
ᴀnn púᴅ, there, yonder.
cᴀoin, gentle.
lonᴣ, a ship.
móp, great.
páippᴅe, a child.

péipc, a reptile.
piᴀn pain.
popc, a fort.
ppoinn, a dinner, a meal.
péipe, a supper.
ull, great.

1. Péipc ᴀ ᴣup ull-ṗéipc. 2. Ull-ṗéipc ᴅuḃ. 3. Ḃi móp-ṗiᴀn opm. 4. Piᴀn ᴀ ᴣup móp-ṗiᴀn. 5. Popc ᴀ ᴣup lonᴣ-ṗopc. 6. Ḃi

lⁱⁿᵹ-ꝑoꞃꞇ ᴀᵹᴀⁱᵬ ᴀⁿⁿ. 7. Ꝑꞃoⁱⁿⁿ ᴀᵹuꞃ ceuᴅ-
ꝑꞃoⁱⁿⁿ. 8. Ꝑꞃoⁱⁿⁿ ᴀᵹuꞃ ꞃéⁱꞃe. 9. Cuⁱꞃ
ceuᴅ-ꝑꞃoⁱⁿⁿ ᴀⁿⁿ ꞃo. 10. Cᴀoⁱⁿ-ꝑáⁱꞃᴅe.

---

1. A reptile and a monster. 2. A black
monster. 3. Great pain was on me. 4. Pain,
and a great pain. 5. A fort and a camp. 6. A
camp was to you there (you had, &c.) 7. Dinner and breakfast. 8. Dinner and supper.
9. Put breakfast here. 10. A gentle child.

EXERCISE VIII. Ṡ.

Ṡ sounds exactly like *h*.

S is never aspirated *before* ᵬ, c, ᴅ, ᵹ, m, ꝑ, ꞇ.

S aspirate never appears at the end of any
word, or in the middle of any word except
compounds.

áꞃᴅ-ꞃcoⁱl, a high school, a college.

móꞃ-ꞃeol, a main-sail.

ꞃíoꞃ (*heeos*), below.

꜒ ꞃuᴀꞃ (*hooas*), above.

ꞇꞃom-ꞃuᴀⁿ, a deep sleep.

ᴀⁿíoꞃ, up.

ᴀⁿuᴀꞃ, down.

ꞃáᵹ, leave.

ꞃᴀⁿ, stay.

oꞃm, on me.

ꞃcoⁱl, a school.

ꞃeol, a sail.

ꞃíoꞃ, down (see obs.)

ꞃuᴀⁿ, rest, sleep.

ꞃuᴀꞃ, up (see obs.)

ꞇᴀꞃ, come.

ꞇꞃom, heavy.

1. Ḃí ṗé ṡuaṗ. 2. Ḃí ṡíḃ ṗíoṗ. 3. Cuiṗ ṡuaṗ é. 4. Cuiṗ ṗíoṗ an leaḃaṗ. 5. Ċaṗ anuaṡ aᵹuṡ ṗan ᴧnn ṗo ṗíoṗ. 6. beiṗ aníoṗ ċuᵹam é aᵹuṡ ṗáᵹ ann ṗo ṡuaṗ é. 7. Ḃí ṡcoil aᵹuṡ áṗo-ṡcoil ann. 8. Seol aᵹuṡ móṗ-ṡeol. 9. Suan aᵹuṡ cṗom-ṡuan. 10. Ḃí cṗom-ṡuan oṗm.

---

1. He was above. 2. Ye were below. 3. Put it up. 4. Put down the book. 5. Come down (from above) and stay below here. 6. Bring it up (from below) to me and leave it above here. 7. (There) were a school and a college there. 8. A sail and a main-sail. 9. Rest and deep sleep. 10. (There) was a deep sleep on me.

OBS.— Motion from above is expressed by anuaṡ, "down" (*from above*). Motion from below by aníoṡ, "up" (*from below*). See Exercise XVIII., *First Book.* A state of rest *above* is expressed by ṡuaṡ, "above;" a similar state below is expressed by ṡíoṡ, " below " (*without motion*), as shown in above Exercise. Síoṡ and ṡuaṡ (ṡ not dotted) are used to imply motion up and down (active).

EXERCISE IX. Ċ.

Ċ also sounds like *h*.

It is faintly sounded *when final*, except when the following word begins with a vowel.

aċaiṗ, a father.
bráċaiṗ (*brawhir*), a brother.
ḟlaiċ, a prince.
ɤo bráċ, forever: bráċ literally signifies "judgment," and hence "ɤo bráċ," i.e. to (the day) of

judgment, means "for ever."
liaċ, gray.
maiċ, good.
máċaiṗ, a mother.
móṗ-ċaṗc, great thirst.
ṗiuċ, a stream.

ceann, a head.
ceann-ċiṗe, a headland.
Eiṗe, Ireland.
ɤan, without

ṗúṗ, a sister.
caṗc, thirst.
cinn, sick.

1. Aċaiṗ maiċ. 2. ɤan aċaiṗ no máċaiṗ. 3. Siúṗ aɤuṗ bráċaiṗ. 4. Ḃi an bráċaiṗ liaċ. 5. Cá buṗ máċaiṗ cinn. 6. Cá móṗ-ċaṗc oṗm. 7. Cá ṗiuċ ann ṗo. 8. Ḃi ceann-ċiṗe ann. 9. Eiṗe ɤo bráċ. 10. Iṗ ḟlaiċ ṗeunṁaṗ é.

1. A good father. 2. Without father or mother. 3. Sister and brother. 4. The brother was gray. 5. Your mother is sick. 6. A great thirst is on me (I am very thirsty). 7. (There) is a stream here. 8. There was a headland there. 9. Ireland for ever. 10. He is a prosperous prince.

OBS.—bráċaiṗ and ṗúṗ may be used for brother and sister in *religion* or as members of the same society. (See Exercise XI.) In Munster bráċaiṗ and ṗúṗ are often used to signify cousins.

There is here an example of an exception to Rule regarding aspiration of initial letter of second portion of a compound word. If the first part of the compound ends in ᴅ, ᴄ, ṙ, ʟ, n, the second part is not aspirated if its initial letter be ᴅ or ᴄ, as in the word " ceᴀnnᴄiṗe" in above Exercise.

EXERCISE X.

This Exercise contains examples of aspir-ated letters nearly silent in the body of words. In some words ᴠ̇ and ᵹ̇ are inserted merely to keep apart, without violating euphony, vowels belonging to different syllables ; otherwise such vowels would run into one syllable to avoid the hiatus that would result from their standing together uncombined. This insertion of adventitious letters is frequently used in the inflections of words.

ᴀiṗiᵹ̇ᴄe, special.	ceᴀnnuiᴠ̇e, a merchant.
ḃᴀoᵹ̇ᴀʟ, danger.	cṗiᴀᴠ̇ᴀiṗe, a labourer.
ḃuᴀᴠ̇ᴀiṗᴄ, trouble.	cṗóᴠ̇ᴀ, valiant.
ḃuíᴠ̇eᴀċ, thankful.	ᵹ̇leoúᴀċ, noisy, quar-
ḃuíᴠ̇eᴀċᴀṗ, thanks,	relsome.
gratitude.	
mé, I, me.	ᴠioᴄ, off thee (*Idiom*, to thee).

1. ḃuíᴠ̇eᴀċᴀṗ leᴀᴄ. 2. ᴄ́ᴀ mé ḃuíᴠ̇eᴀċ ᴠ̇ioᴄ.[1] 3. ḃi ḃuᴀᴠ̇ᴀiṗᴄ oṗm. 4. ḃi ṗé ᵹ̇leoúᴀċ. 5. iṗ cṗóᴠ̇ᴀ ᴀn lᴀoċ é. 6. ᴄ́ᴀ ḃᴀoᵹ̇ᴀl ᴀnn ṗo. 7. iṗ mᴀiᴄ̇ ᴀn cṗiᴀᴠ̇ᴀiṗe é. 8. ḃᴀoᵹ̇ᴀl ᴀᵹuṗ ḃuᴀᴠ̇ᴀiṗᴄ. 9. ḃuíᴠ̇eᴀċᴀṗ ᴀiṗiᵹ̇ᴄe leᴀṗ. 10. Ceᴀnnuiᴠ̇e ᴀᵹuṗ cṗiᴀᴠ̇ᴀiṗe.

[1] ᴠ in ᴠᴀm, ᴠuiᴄ, ᴠioᴄ, &c., is generally aspirated when the preceding word ends in a vowel or aspirated consonant. See page 37.

18 ASPIRATION.

1. Thanks with you. 2. I am thankful tᴏ you. 3. Trouble was on me. 4. He was quarrelsome. 5. He is a valiant warrior. 6. (There) is danger here. 7. He is a good labourer. 8. Danger and trouble. 9. Special thanks with you. 10. A merchant and a husbandman.

EXERCISE XI.

This Exercise contains a few more difficult words in which two aspirate letters come together.

cᴀċ-ḃáṗṗ (*cah-vaar*), a helmet (cᴀċ, a battle, ḃáṗṗ, top or head).

clȯ-ḃuᴀilċe, printed (clȯ, type, and buᴀil, strike).

ᴅeᴀṗḃṗáċᴀiṗ (*dhrawhir*), a brother (ᴅeᴀṗḃ, real, and ḃṗáċᴀiṗ, a brother), a real brother, as distinguished from a brother in religion or society.

ᴅeᴀṗḃṗúṗ (*dherehyure*), a sister, a real sister.

leᴀċ-ṁᴀṗḃ, half dead (leᴀċ and mᴀṗḃ).

loḃċᴀ (*lov-ha*), rotten.

luᴀċṁᴀṗ, precious.

luiḃ-ꙅoṗċ, a herb garden (luiḃ and ꙅoṗċ).

nᴀoṁċᴀ, holy.

neᴀṁċᴀiṗḃeᴀċ (*nye-harvagh*), unprofitable (neᴀṁ, *un*, and ċᴀiṗḃeᴀċ).

ṗᴀiᴏ̇ḃiṗ (*sy-vir*), rich, fertile.

uḃᴀll-ꙅoṗċ, an orchard, i.e., an apple garden (uḃᴀll and ꙅoṗċ).

báɲɲ, top.   lúbċa, looped, bent.
buaıl, strike.   luıb, a herb, a plant.
caċ, a battle.   maɲb, dead.
cloò, type, a nail. ✗ neaṁ (*un, in*), not (nega-
oeaɲb, real.   tive particle).
ouıne, a man, a person. caıɲbeaċ, profitable.
ᵹoɲc a garden, a field. uball, an apple.
leaċ half.

1. bí ɼé lúbċa. 2. bí ɼé lobċa. 3. bí ɲ́
leaċmaɲb. 4. ouıne naomċa. 5. leabaɲ
luaċmaɲ. 6. leabaɲ cloòbuaılce. 7. uball
maıċ aᵹuɼ uball-ᵹoɲc ɼaıòbıɲ. 8. uball-
ᵹoɲc aᵹuɼ luıb-ᵹoɲc neaṁ-caıɲbeaċ. 9. bí
caċ-báɲɲ aıɲ an laoċ. 10. oeaɲbɼıúɲ aᵹuɼ
oeaɲbɼáċaıɲ.

---

1 It was looped. 2. It was rotten. 3. She
was half dead. 4. A holy man. 5. A precious
book. 6. A printed book. 7. A good apple
and a rich orchard. 8. An orchard and an
unprofitable herb garden. 9. (There) was a
helᐧmet on the warrior. 10. A (real) sister
and brother.

OBS.—A few other compounds are here shown. The
learner will, with little difficulty, be able to pronounce them
by attending to the foregoing Rules and Exercises on aspirates final and initial. The aspirate letters, though in some
cases quiescent, or nearly so, are retained in spelling, since,
if rejected, the etymology of the word would be lost, and the
orthography unsettled and without rule.

EXERCISE XII.

THE NUMERALS UP TO TEN.

Cardinal.	*Ordinal.*
ᵈon, one.	ċeuᵈ, ᵈonṁaᵈ, first.
ᵈó, ᵈá, two.	ᵈapa, second.
τpí, three.	τpeap, third.
ceaċaıp, ceıτpe, four.	ceaτpaṁaᵈ, fourth.
cúıᵹ, five.	cúıᵹeaᵈ, fifth.
pé, six.	peıpeaᵈ, sixth.
peaċτ, seven.	peaċτṁaᵈ, seventh.
oċτ, eight.	oċτṁaᵈ, eighth.
naoı, nine.	naoṁaᵈ, ninth.
ᵈeıċ, ten.	ᵈeaċṁaᵈ, tenth.
ba, cows (*plu.* of bó).	lá, a day.
bean, a woman.	mná, women (*plu.* of
bó, a cow.	bean).
bpóᵹ, a shoe.	páın, a spade (*dat.*)
bpóᵹa, shoes.	pán, a spade.
cop, a foot.	pın, that.

1. ᵈon lá.   2. Sın é an ᵈó.   3. An ᵈá páın.
4. τpí bpóᵹa.   5. Ceaċaıp aᵹup cúıᵹ.   6.
Ceıτpe mná.   7. na cúıᵹ ba.   8. An ċeuᵈ
leaḃap.   9. An ᵈapa cop.   10. An τpeap lá.

---

1. One day.   2. That is (the) two.   3. The
two spades.   4. Three shoes.   5. Four and
five.   6. Four women.   7. The five cows.
8. The first book.   9. The second foot.   10.
The third day.

Obs.—Dó and ceaṫair are used without a noun.

Dá and ceiṫre precede and qualify nouns.

Dá requires the article and noun in the *singular* number, if masc. *nominative*, if fem. *dative*, as in example 3; but the adjective which qualifies it is plural. The other numbers given above take the plural, except, of course, aon.

When cardinal numbers are used *without* a noun they require the article to be expressed *except in counting*.

All ordinal numbers require the article.

The c in ċeud, first, is aspirated.

The d in ḋá, two, is often aspirated, chiefly when the preceding word ends in a vowel or aspirated consonant, or when ḋá is the first word of a sentence.

EXERCISE XIII.

THE NUMERALS FROM ELEVEN TO TWENTY.

aon-deug, eleven.
dó-ḋeug or dá-deug, twelve.
trí-deug, thirteen.
ceaṫair-deug, or ceiṫre-deug, fourteen.
cúig-deug, fifteen.
sé-deug, sixteen.
seaċt-deug, seventeen.
oċt-deug, eighteen.
naoi-deug, nineteen.
fiċe, twenty.

aonṁaḋ-deug, eleventh.
dara-deug, twelfth.
treas-deug, thirteenth.
ceaṫraṁaḋ-deug, fourteenth.
cúigeaḋ-deug, fifteenth.
seiseaḋ-deug, sixteenth.
seaċtṁaḋ-deug, seventeenth.
oċtṁaḋ-deug, eighteenth.
naoṁaḋ-deug, nineteenth.
fiċeaḋ, twentieth.

ál, a brood. eun, a bird. mí, a month.

1. Αοn lá οeuꝧ. 2. Θá lá οeuꝧ. 3. Αn
ceαċαιρ-οeuꝧ. 4. Αn cúιꝧeαϋ mí οeuꝧ. 5.
Ϝιċe coρ. 6. Αn ριċeαϋ ϝeαρ. 7. Αn οá eun
αꝧuρ αn ꞇρeαρ ál. 8. Αn cúιꝧeαϋ lá οeuꝧ
αꝧuρ αn ριċeαϋ mí. 9. Ϙeιċ mná αꝧuρ ϝιċe
ϝeαρ. 10. Αn ριċe ϝeαρ.

---

1. Eleven days. 2. Twelve days. 3. (The)
fourteen. 4. The fifteenth month. 5. Twenty
feet. 6. The twentieth man. 7. The two
birds and the third brood. 8. The fifteenth
day and the twentieth month. 9 Ten women
and twenty men. 10. The twenty men.

OBS.—Ϙeuꝧ (for Ϙeιċ) is equivalent to the English " teen"
(from ten). When a number greater than ten, composed of
a simple numeral and Ϙeuꝧ is expressed, the noun is placed
between the number and Ϙeuꝧ as above.

Ϝιċe, and all the multiples of Ϙeιċ, take the noun in the
singular number.

EXERCISE XIV.

The following sentences contain only words
previously used, and will form a simple and
useful Exercise on the mutable letters and their
sounds, as shown in the foregoing Exercises.
A translation is unnecessary. All the words
used are given at the end of the book.

αċꞇ, but.   má, if.
αꝧαꞇ, at thee.   ρραρán, a purse.
ιαο, they, them.

A

1. Bí an ḋaṁ agus an fiaḋ fuaḋ.
2. Bí an maḋaḋ fuaḋ, agus an luċ liaṫ.
3. Bí an ḋá eun buiḋe agus an fiaċ duḃ.
4. Ḋá laoġ agus fice geaṁfiaḋ.
5. Aon uillpéirt aṁáin agus péirt duḃ.
6. Muc agus mart, daṁ agus tarḃ.
7. Bí caoiri-ḟeoil maoirt-ḟeoil agus muic-ḟeoil agaiḃ.
8. Bí gaḃair agaiḃ ann fin, agus laoġ buiḋe.
9. Mile buiḋeaċar leat, agus aḋ agus róġ oirt.
10. Bí riḃ buiḋeaċ díom.

B

1. Cuir an maḋaḋ amaċ.
2. Bí buir leanḃ aétiġ, agus bí ruan air.
3. Beir na bróga airteaċ ċugam ann ro.
4. Bí ré amuiġ, agus bí móir-pian air.
5. Bí an reaḋn-ḟeaḃ liaċ.
6. Bí móir-ċart oirm, agus bí trom-ḟuan air.
7. Bí an feaḃr gairḃ, agus bí caċ-báirr air.
8. Ir anaṁ bí ré air rcoil, aċt tá ré air aro-rcoil anoir.
9. Ir luiḃ-ġoirt neaṁṫoirḃeaċ é, aċt ir uḃall-ġoirt raidḃir é.
10. Bí poirt agus longpoirt agaiḃ.

C

1. Cuip puap an leabap cloṫ-buailce.
2. Tá baoġal agup buaṫaipc ann po píop.
3. beip píop pice aṫapc, agup fáġ pice caċ. bápp puap.
4. Tap anuap ċuġam, agup pan ann po píop
5. beip aníop ċuġam na bpóġa agup fáġ puap iaṫ.
6. bí an láṁ lán, aċc bí an ppapán pollaṁ.
7. bí an leabap naoṁċa, luaċṁap, agup bí apṫ-ṁeap aip.
8. bí an leanb ġleoṫaċ, agup bí an aṫapc lúbċa.
9. bí an cloċaipe caoċ, agup an ceapnuíṫe leaċ-ṁapb.
10. bí poiġiṫ agup ġráṫ aġ an naoṁ.

D

1. An é an ṫó, no an ceaċaip, no an cúiġ?
2. Ṫeiċ mná, ṫá eaċ ṫeuġ agup pice caopa.
3. bí cpí míle eaċ ann púṫ agup cúiġ céaṫ laoċ.
4. An ṫapa lá ṫeuġ agup an piceaṫ mí.
5. bí naoi mná agup ṫá leanb ṫeuġ ann.
6. bí an ṫeaċṁaṫ cloċ aġaib.
7. bí ceicpe bpóġa aġaib.
8. áṫmuṫ lobċa agup uball maiċ.

9. Ⅽá ṗaóaṗc ȝeuṗ maiⅽ aȝainn.
10. Ḃí cṗoíóe cṗóóa aȝuṗ aȝaió ḟeaṗaṁail aȝ an laoċ.

E

1. Aⅽaiṗ aȝuṗ máⅽaiṗ, ꝺeaṗḃṗúṗ aȝuṗ ꝺeaṗḃṗáⅽaiṗ.
2. ꝺeaṗḃṗáⅽaiṗ aȝuṗ bṗáⅽaiṗ, ꝺeaṗḃṗúṗ aȝuṗ ṗúṗ.
3. Ceuꝺ-ṗṗoinn aȝuṗ ṗṗoinn aȝuṗ ṗéiṗe.
4. Ḃí an ⅽalaṁ maiⅽ aȝuṗ ḃí an cṗaóaiṗo ṗeunṁaṗ.
5. Ḃí an ꝺeaȝ-ṗíȝ ṗean aȝuṗ ḃí an ḟlaiⅽ cṗóóa.
6. Ⅽá aon loċ ꝺeuȝ aȝuṗ ṗíċe ṗṗuⅽ aȝuṗ ceann-ⅽiṗe annṗin.
7. Ⅽá ṗioṗ-ċaṗa ṗeaṗṁaċ aȝuṗ ṗioṗ-ḃuan aȝam.
8. Ⅽṗeun-ḟeaṗ aȝuṗ ṗaoṗ-óuine.
9. Ṁá ⅽá ⅽiṗ-ȝṗáó aȝaⅽ, ḟóȝluim ȝaeóilȝe.
10. ' Eiṗe ȝo bṗáⅽ.

SECTION II.

Euphony is the basis on which the affected sounds of the mutable consonants rest. In order to prevent the confusion which would arise from letters being changed in sound according to the ideas of euphony prevailing in different districts, and even among different individuals, it is clear that the changes of these letters, and the positions in which they suffer change, must be regulated by some system. In showing the secondary sounds of these letters in the preceding exercises, we merely used the aspirated letters in words to which they essentially belong, and where they may be said in some sense to fill the place of additional letters like *v, w*, &c. We now come to treat of them in cases where the initial letter, which in one instance has its natural sound, in another instance changes that sound into a kindred one (as b into *v*), when influenced by certain parts of speech expressed or under‐ stood before it. The system which Irish grammarians have laid down for the regulation of these changes is contained in the following rules, which, although belonging to Grammar proper, are here given in order that the learner may fully understand this subject.

In the succeeding Exercises some inflected forms of nouns and verbs will be met with, but we shall not here enter upon declension or conjugation. All such forms will be ex‐ plained as they occur ; but to enter fully into the rules regarding them would, at this stage, be premature. The rules regarding gender are also held over, but the gender of each word is shown in the vocabulary at the end of the book.

RULES FOR ASPIRATION.

RULE I.

THE Article ᴀn, *the*, causes aspiration of the initial consonant (if aspirable) of *feminine* nouns in the nominative and accusative cases ; as beᴀn, a woman, ᴀn ḃeᴀn, the woman.

EXERCISE I.

Examples of Feminine Nouns as influenced by the Article.

ᴀn ḃeᴀn, the woman.
ᴀn ḃᴀın-ḟeıp, the wed-
  ding.
ᴀn ḃeᴀċᴀ, the life.
ᴀn ḃlıᴀ́ḋᴀın, the year.
ᴀn ḃó, the cow.
ᴀn ċᴀċᴀıp, the city.
ᴀn ċloċ, the stone.
ᴀn ċolᴀnn, the body.
ᴀn ḟᴀıpᵹe, the sea.

ᴀn ḟuınneoᵹ, the win-
  dow.
ᴀn ᵹᴀoċ, the wind.
ᴀn ṁᴀıoın, the morning.
ᴀn   ṁᴀıᵹoeᴀn,   the
  maiden.
ᴀn ṁᴀċᴀıp, the mother.
ᴀn ṁın, the meal.
ᴀn póᵹ, the kiss.
ᴀn ṗpoınn, the dınneᴄ

EXERCISE II.

ᴀopᴏᴀ, aged.
cᴀıċ, eat, spend.
oeᴀpᵹ, red.

ᵹlᴀc, take, receive.
lᴀıoıp, strong.
mín, fine.

1. Cᴀ́ ᴀn ḃeᴀn ᴀopᴏᴀ.   2. 1p mᴀıċ ᴀn ḃlıᴀ́ḋᴀın í po.   3. Cᴀ́ ᴀn ḃó oeᴀpᵹ.   4. Ḃı ᴀp

ċaċaip móp. 5. Cá an ċloċ luaċṁap. 6. Cá
an ḟaipʒe láiṁip. 7. Cá an ʒaoċ ʒapḃ.
8. Cá an ṁin min. 9. Cá an ṁaiṁin bpeáʒ.
10. Caiċ an ḟpoinn.

---

1. The woman is aged. 2. This is a good
year. 3. The cow is red. 4. The city was
large. 5. The stone is precious. 6. The sea
is strong. 7. The wind is rough. 8. The
meal is fine. 9. The morning is fine. 10. Eat
the dinner.

Obs.—Feminine nouns beginning with ꝺ or c are not influenced by the article, as an ceine *the fire*, the sound of n in
an being sufficiently euphonius with these letters. Beginning
with p, they are not aspirated, but suffer a change which will
be explained when treating of Eclipsis.

The learner will remember that p before b,
c, ꝺ, ʒ, m, p, c, cannot be aspirated, as an
ppeal, *the scythe*.

RULE II.

The article causes aspiration of the initial
consonant (if aspirable) of *masculine* nouns ir
the genitive case singular ; an baile, the town,
an ḃaile, of the town.

bápꝺ, a bard.　　　　peap, a man.
buċaill, a cowboy.　　pion, wine.
capall, a horse.　　　pocal, a word.
caċ, a battle.　　　　manaċ, a monk.
cláp, a table.　　　　pobal, a people

EXERCISE III.

Examples of genitive case of Masculine Nouns as influenced by the Article.

an baile, of the town.	an fíona, of the wine.
an báipo, of the bard.	an fip, of the man.
an buacalla, of the cowboy.	an focail, of the word.
an capaill, of the horse.	an gnó, of the work.
an cata, of the battle.	an gaduide, of the thief.
an cipoe, of the chest.	an mála, of the bag.
an cláip, of the table.	an manaig of the monk.
	an pobail, of the people.

EXERCISE IV.

cleap, craft. X	mac, a son.
doipn, a fist.	óp, gold.
glap, a lock.	ppáio, a street.
lán, the full.	teac, a house.
log, a hollow.	

1 Ppáio an baile. 2. Mac an báipo.
3. Doipn an buacalla. 4. Log an cata.
5. Glap an cipoe. 6. Cop an fip. 7. Cleap
an gaduide. 8. Lán an mála. 9. Teac an
manaig. 10. Óp an pobail.

---

1. (The) street of the town. 2. (The) Son
of the bard. 3. (The) Fist of the cowboy.

4. (The) Hollow of the battle. 5. (The) Lock of the chest. 6. (The) Foot of the man. 7. (The) Craft of the thief. 8. (The) Full of the bag. 9. (The) House of the monk. 10. (The) Gold of the people.

Obs.—Nouns beginning with ꝺ, ꞇ, or ꞅ, are exceptions. (See observations on Rule I.)

RULE III.

COMPOUND WORDS.

In compound words, no matter from what parts of speech they are formed, the initial letter of the second part is aspirated, if it be of the aspirable class. Some examples have been already shown in preceding Exercises.[*]

EXERCISE V.

Examples of Compound Words.

cloᵹ-ċeaċ, a bell-house.
ꝺeaᵹ-ꝺuine, a good-man.
ꝼaol-ċú, a wolf (*wild-dog*).
ꝼioꞃ-ḃuan, steadfast.
ꝼioꞃ-ṫílıꞃ, sincere.
laoıᵹ-ꝼeoıl, veal (*calf-flesh*).
ꞅean-ḃean, an old woman.

[*] See Obs. at end of this Exercise.

ᴀᴘᴛᴏ-ᴘíᵹ, a monarch, a high-king.
bᴀɪn-ᴘíoᵹᴀn,[1] a queen (i.e., *a woman-king*).
bᴀɪn-ᴛɪᵹeᴀᴘnᴀ, a lady (i.e., *a woman-lord*).
buᴀn-ᴘᴀoᵹᴀlᴀc, long-lived.
buᴀn-ᴘeᴀᴘᵐᴀc, persevering (*lasting-firm*)

EXERCISE VI.

ᴀᴘᴘᴀ, ancient.
Éᴘeᴀnn, of Ireland (genitive of Éᴘe).
uᴀᴘᴀl, noble.

1. ᴀn ᴘíᵹ ᴀᵹuᴘ ᴀn bᴀɪn-ᴘíoᵹᴀn.   2. ᴀᴘᴛᴏ-
ᴘíᵹ ᴀᵹuᴘ bᴀɪn-ᴛɪᵹeᴀᴘnᴀ.   3. bᴀɪn-ᴘíoᵹᴀn
Éᴘeᴀnn.   4. ᴀn ᴘᴀol-cú ᴀᵹuᴘ ᴀn ᵹeᴀᴘᴘ-ᴘɪᴀᴛᴏ.
5. ᴛᴏeᴀᵹ-ᴛᴏuɪne nᴀoᵐᴛᴀ.   6. ᴛɪᴘ-ᵹᴘᴀᴛᴏ buᴀn-
ᴘeᴀᴘᵐᴀc.   7. bɪ ᴀn ᴘlᴀɪᴛ buᴀn-ᴘᴀoᵹᴀlᴀc.
8. Cloᵹ-ᴛeᴀc ᴀᴘᴘᴀ.   9. ᴛᴀ ᴀn bᴀɪn-ᴛɪᵹeᴀᴘnᴀ
uᴀᴘᴀl.   10. ᴛᴀ ᴀn ᴛᴏeᴀᵹ-ᴛᴏuɪne ᴘᴀɪᴛᴏbɪᴘ.

---

1. The king and the queen. 2. A monarch
and a lady. 3. Queen of Ireland. 4. The
wolf and the hare. 5. A holy good man.
6. Persevering patriotism. 7. The prince was
long-lived. 8. An ancient bell-house. 9. The
lady is noble. 10. The good man is rich.

Obs.—When the first part of a compound ends in ᴛᴏ, ᴛ, ᴘ,
l, or n, and the second begins with ᴛᴏ or ᴛ, the latter is not
aspirated. This Rule is entirely based on Euphony. Prac-
tice is the best guide to show when the aspirate is required
to make the two words unite smoothly.

[1] bᴀn is a feminine prefix. It is spelled bᴀɪn when the
following vowel is slender.

Exercise VII.

Where the latter part of a compound word is in the genitive case no aspiration takes place. Several instances occurred in the *First Book*, and an Exercise is now given on words of this kind.

ᴀill, a cliff.	✗ ᵹᴀil, vapour.
ᴀ́ᵱᴅ, high, loud.	ᵹlic, wise.
ceol, music.	iᴀᵱᴀn, iron.
coᵹᴀᴛ́, war.	muiᵱ, sea.
ᴅonn, brown.	ceine, fire.
ᵱoᵱ, knowledge.	uiᵱᵹe, water.

cú-mᴀᵱᴀ (dog of the sea), a sea-dog.
ᵱeᴀᵱ-ceoil (man of music), a musician.
ᵱeᴀᵱ-ᵱeᴀᵱᴀ (man of knowledge), a seer, wizard.
lᴀoᵹ-mᴀᵱᴀ (calf of the sea), a seal.
lonᵹ-coᵹᴀiᴛ́, a ship of war.
lonᵹ-ᵹᴀile (boat of vapour), a steamboat.
obᴀiᵱ-ceine (work of fire), a fire-work.

bóċᴀᵱ-iᴀᵱᴀin (road of iron), a railroad.
mᴀc-ᴀllᴀ (son of the cliff), an echo.
obᴀiᵱ-uiᵱᵹe (work of water), a water-work.

1. Cᴀ ᴀn bóċᴀᵱ-iᴀᵱᴀin ᴀnn ᵱo ᴀnoiᵱ. 2. ᴃi ᴀn lonᵹ-ᵹᴀile lᴀ́n. 3. Cᴀ́ ᴀn lonᵹ-coᵹᴀiᴛ́ ᵱollᴀṁ. 4. ᴃi ᴀn ᵱeᴀᵱ-ᵱeᴀᵱᴀ ᵹlic. 5. ᴀn ᵱeᴀᵱ-ceoil ᴀᵹuᵱ ᴀn ᵱeᴀᵱ-ᵱeᴀᵱᴀ. 6. Obᴀiᵱ-ceine ᴀᵹuᵱ oᴮ⸱ᴀiᵱ-uiᵱᵹe. 7. ᴃi ᴀn lᴀoᵹ-mᴀᵱᴀ ᴅonn. 8. ᴀ⸱ ιlonᵹ-coᵹᴀiᴛ́ ᴀᵹuᵱ ᴀn lonᵹ-ᵹᴀile. 9. ᴃi ᴀn mᴀc-ᴀllᴀ ᴀ́ᵱᴅ. 10. Cú-mᴀnᴀ ᴅuᴃ.

1. The railroad is here now. 2. The steamboat was full. 3. The man-of-war is empty.
4. The seer was wise. 5. The musician and
the seer. 6. A fire-work and a water-work.
7. The seal was brown. 8. The man-of-war
and the steamboat. 9. The echo was loud
(high). 10. A black sea-dog.

RULE IV.

PROPER NAMES.

When the latter of two nouns is a proper
name in the genitive case it suffers aspiration,
if the article be not expressed.

EXERCISE VIII.

ᴀιmγιp, time.	Mιċιl, of Michael.
ᴀγroᵹᴀγpoᵹ, an arch-bishop.	muιnᴄιp, people.
bγιᵹιᴅ, Brigid.	Pᴀopᴀιc, Patrick.
bγιᵹᴅe, of Brigid.	Peᴀᴅᴀp, Peter.
Cᴀιᴄιlín, Catherine.	Peᴀᴅᴀιp, of Peter.
Copcᴀċ, Cork.	Popᴄlᴀιpᵹe, Waterford.
Copcᴀιᵹe, of Cork.	rúιl, an eye.
ιnᵹeᴀn, a daughter.	Comᴀr, Thomas.
Mᴀιpe, Mary.	Comᴀιr, of Thomas.
Mιċeᴀl, Michael.	Cuᴀm, Tuam.
	Cuᴀmᴀ, of Tuam.

Examples.

1. 'Ároeaſpoʒ Ċuama. 2. Aimſiſ ṗáoſaic. 3. Inʒeán Ċomáiſ. 4. bean ṁicil.
5. muinciſ Ċoſcaiʒe. 6. mac ṁáiſe.
7. Ceaċ Caiċilín. 8. Súil Ḃſiʒoe. 9. Caċaiſ
ṗoſcláiſʒe. 10. Capall ṗeaoaiſ.

---

1. Archbishop of Tuam. 2. (The) time of
Patrick. 3. Thomas's daughter. 4. Michael's
wife. 5. (The) people of Cork. 6. Mary's son.
7. Catherine's house. 8. Brigid's eye. 9. (The)
City of Waterford. 10. Peter's horse.

EXERCISE IX.

Exception.

Family names following " o " or " ua " (descendant), and " mac" (son), though *always* in
the genitive case, do not suffer aspiration, but
after " ní " (daughter), they do.

OBS.—1. But these names suffer aspiration when "mac"
means literally a "*son*," and "ua," an actual "*grandson*,"
and not a descendant, as a member of a clan.

2. Also these names are aspirated when they follow the
genitive case of these prefixes (uí of a descendant, mic of a
son. The following Exercise shows these peculiarities.

3. These names are aspirated when they follow the genitive case of the prefix maol, often used after "o" in family
names, as O'maoil bſenoain, or ʒiolla after mac, as mac
ʒiolla ṗáoſaic. maol here signifies a *votary*, and ʒiolla
a *disciple*, thus " the descendant of the votary of Breudau," or
the "son of the disciple of Patrick"

bṗian, Brian.   Oóṁnaill, of Daniel.
bṗiain, of Brian.   Caóg, Teig, Thaddeus.
Oóṁnall, Daniel.   Caióg, of Teig.

1. Comáṗ mac Caióg. 2. Comáṗ Mac Caióg
3. páopaic ua bṗiain. 4. páopaic O'bṗiain
5. Oóṁnall O'Connaill. 6. Mac Oóṁnaill
Ui Connaill. 7. Comáṗ O'Goṗmain. 8. bean
Comáiṗ Ui Goṗmain. 9. Máiṗe Ni bṗiain.
10. Inġean Máiṗe Ni bṗiain.

---

1. Thomas, son of Teig (Rule IV. and Obs.
1). 2. Thomas Mac Teig (excep.). 3. Patrick,
grandson of Brian (Rule IV. and Obs 1).
4. Patrick O'Brien (exception). 5. Daniel
O'Connell (exception). 6. Son of (Rule IV.)
Daniel O'Connell (Obs. 2). 7. Thomas O'Gorman. 8. Wife of (Rule IV.) Thomas O'Gorman.
9. Mary O'Brien (" ni," see exception).
10. Daughter of (Rule IV.) Mary O'Brien.

OBS.—1. The learner has here some examples of family
names. The prefix " O " or Ua " signifies—1st, a "grandson" (as in Example 3, above); 2nd, a "descendant," or
member of a family claiming a common ancestor (as in
Examples 4 and 5). Mac signifies a "son," and is also
prefixed to the name of an ancestor to form a family name. It
follows the same rules as "Ua."
2. "Ua" and "Mac" being the prefixes for names of
males, "Ni" (contracted for "Inġean," a "daughter") is
used for female names, since it is clear we could not say
Máiṗe Mac Caṗṫaig (i.e., son of Caṗṫaċ) though used
ignorantly in English

RULE V.

ADJECTIVES.

Adjectives beginning with mutable consonants and agreeing with the nouns which
they qualify are aspirated in the following instances :

1st, In the nominative and accusative
singular *feminine.*
2nd, In the genitive singular *masculine.*
3rd, In the vocative singular of both genders, and in the dative.

EXERCISE X.

Examples of First Instance.

ailł ġeal, a white cliff.
bó bán, a white cow.
bróġ ḟaiprinġ, a wide
shoe.
cor ḟaoa, a long foot.
cuirle ḋearġ, a red vein.
oair ġarb, a rugged oak.
opireoġ ġlar, a green
brier.
ḟeoil ṁaiṫ, good meat.

puinneoġ ḟorġailte,
an open window.
léim ṁór, a great leap.
maroin bréáġ, a fine
morning.
rġian ġeup, a sharp
knife.
cír ḟeunṁar, a pros-
perous country.

EXERCISE XI.

1. An ḟeoil ṁaiṫ. 2. An ċor ḟaoa ṁór.
3. An bróġ ḟaiprinġ. 4. An oair ġarb.

5. An¹ ᵲᵹιᴀn ᵹeuᵲ. 6. An bó ᴏᴠb. 7. Iᵲ
mᴀιᴏιn ᴀluιnn bᵲeᴀᵹ í. 8. Ċιᵲ ᵰᴀιᴏbιᵲ
ᵰeunṁᴀᵲ. 9. Ꭺιll ᵹeᴀl ṁóᵲ. 10. Ċᴀ ᵰuιn·
nᴇoᵹ ᵰoᵲᵹᴀιlᴄe ᴀnn. ͡ ͡

---

1. The good meat. 2. The long big foot.
3. The wide shoe. 4. The rough oak. 5. The
sharp knife. 6. The black cow. 7. It is a
beautiful fine morning. 8. A rich prosperous
country. 9. A great white cliff. 10. (There)
is an open window there.

OBS.—ᴏ and ᴄ are excepted if the noun ends in n, and
sometimes before a broad vowel.
The adjective is seldom aspirated in the plural.
For the sake of Euphony the " ᴏ " in " ᴏᴀm," " ᴏuιᴄ," and
other prepositional pronouns, is generally aspirated whenever
the preceding word ends in a vowel or an aspirated conson·
ant.—See note, page 17.

EXERCISE XII.

bᴀn, white.	cᴀᴄ, a cat.
beo, } living.	ceol. music.
bí, (gen.) } living.	ᵲuᴀᵲ, cold.
bᵲeᴀc, speckled.	móᵲ, large.

Examples of Second Instance.

bᴀιle ṁóιᵲ, of a large town.
cᴀιᴄ bᵲιc, of a speckled cat.
cᴀpᴀιll bᴀιn, of a white horse.
ceoιl bιnn, of harmonious music.
ᴏuιlle ṁóιᵲ, of a large leaf.

¹ See Rule I., and Obs. on ᴏ and ᴄ, and ᵲ before mutes,
page 28.

duine ḋona, of an unfortunate man.
duine ḟona, of a fortunate man.
fáinne ḃuiḋe, of a yellow ring.
fíona ḋeirg, of red wine.
fir ḃí, of a living man.
fir ṁóir, of a big man.
scoláire ċliste, of an expert scholar.
tíġearna ċróḋa, of a valiant chieftain.
tobair ḟuair, of a cold well.
uisge ṁilis, of sweet water.

Exercise XIII.

blas, taste.	eolas, knowledge.
ceann, a head.	sráid, a street.
cluas, an ear.	srian, a bridle.

1. Sráid an ḃaile ṁóir. 2. Cluas capaill ḃáin. 3. Leanḃ an ḟir ṁóir. 4. Eolas an scoláire ċliste. 5. Fuaim an ċeoil ḃinn. 6. Blas uisge ṁilis. 7. Ceann an duine ṁóir. 8. Uisge tobair ḟuair. 9. 'Aḋ an duine ḋona. 10. Sóġ an duine ḟona.

---

1. (The) street of the large town. 2. (The) ear of a white horse. 3. (The) child of the big man. 4. (The) knowledge of the expert scholar. 5. (The) sound of the harmonious music. 6. (The) taste of sweet water. 7. (The) head of the big man. 8. Water of a cold well. 9. (The) luck of the unfortunate man. 10. (The) pleasure of the fortunate man.

Exercises on the *third* instance of this Rule, nouns and adjectives aspirated in the *dative*, are held over till we come to treat of the influence of prepositions (Rule XII., page 51), which are always used with that case. Exercises on nouns and adjectives aspirated in the *vocative* are held over till we treat of the sign of that case under interjections (Rule XIII., page 53).

NOTE.—The nominative plural masculine of adjectives is often aspirated when the preceding noun ends in a consonant.

Examples.

fip ṁópa, big men.
pocail caoṁa, gentle words.
leinb flána, healthy children.
uplaip cioṗma, dry floors.

RULE VI.

The following numeral adjectives cause aspiration, viz.:—The cardinal numbers aon (one), and vá (two), and their compounds, and the ordinal numbers ceuv, cpeap.

EXERCISE XIV.

1. An ceuv feap. 2. Vá fáinne. 3. Aon páipoc vcug. 4. An ceuv bliavain. 5. Vá feap veug. 6. Aon capall veug. 7. An cpeap ṁí veug. 8. Vá feap aguf veic mná.

9. Ɑon ṁac ꝺeuʒ.   10. Ɑn ċeuꝺ ḟeaṗ aʒuṛ an cṗeaṛ ḃeɑn.

---

1. The first man. 2. Two rings. 3. Eleven children. 4. The first year. 5. Twelve men. 6. Eleven horses. 7. The thirteenth month. 8. Two men and ten women. 9. Eleven sons. 10. The first man and the third woman.

The learner will refer to Exercise XII. (Section I.), on the numbers. Ɑon does not aspirate before ꝺ or c. (See Obs. on Rule I.).

RULE VII.
PRONOUNS.

The possessive pronouns, mo (my), ꝺo (thy), a (his), cause aspiration of the initial consonants (if aspirable) of the nouns before which they are placed.

EXERCISE XV.
Examples.

a ḃṛáċaiṗ, his brother. a ṁuinciṗ, his people.
mo ċuiṛle, my pulse.   ꝺo ṗáiṛꝺe, thy child.
a ꝺoṗn, his fist.   ꝺo ṫṗón, thy nose.
a ḟeaṗann, his field.   mo ċeanʒa, my tongue.
a ḟuil, his blood.   mo ċíṗ, my country.
ꝺo ṁáċaiṗ, thy mother.

EXERCISE XVI.

When mo and ʋo are followed by a vowel the o is omitted, and an apostrophe inserted to mark its absence, also before the letter ꝼ. as m' ᴀċᴀıꝗ, my father; m' ꝼuıl, my blood.

ʋúnċᴀ, shut.   óᴣ, young.
ıonṁuın, dear.   ꝗlán, well, healthy.

1. ꝳo bꝗáċᴀıꝗ ıonṁuın. 2. Ċá m' ᴀċᴀıꝗ ꝗlán. 3. bi m' ꝼuıl ʋeᴀꝗᴣ. 4. Ċá ᴀ ʋoꝗn ʋúnċᴀ. 5. ʋoꝛáıꝛʋe óᴣ. 6. bi ᴀ ṁuınċıꝗ ꝗᴀıʋbıꝗ. 7. ꝳo ċıꝗ ᴀᴣuꝛ mo ṁuınċıꝗ. 8. ᴀ ᴀċᴀıꝗ ᴀᴣuꝛ ᴀ ṁáċᴀıꝗ. 9. bi mo ꝛáıꝛʋe ᴀꝗċıᴣ ᴀċċ bi ʋo bꝗáċᴀıꝗ ᴀmuıᴣ. 10. ꝳo ċuıꝗle ᴀᴣuꝛ mo ᴣꝗáʋ.

———

1. My dear brother. 2. My father is well. 3. My blood was red. 4. His fist is shut. 5. Thy young child. 6. His people were rich. 7. My country and my people. 8. His father and his mother. 9. My child was in, but your brother was outside. 10. My pulse and my love.

ᴀ (her) causes no change, except before vowels, as will be shown in Rules of Eclipsis. ᴀ (their), ᴀꝗ (our), and buꝗ (your), will also be treated of under Eclipsis.

For aspiration with relative pronoun, see Rule X., page 46.

RULE VIII.

VERBS.

Verbs beginning with a mutable consonant are aspirated in the infinitive mood by the particles ᴅo or ᴀ.

EXERCISE XVII.

Examples.

ᴅo or ᴀ, ƀuᴀlᴀᴅ, to strike.

ᴅo or ᴀ, ċoᴦ5, to check.

ᴅo or ᴀ, ċuᴘ, to put.

ᴅo or ᴀ, ᴅeunᴀᴅ, to do.

ᴅo or ᴀ, ᴅúnᴀᴅ, to shut.

ᴅo or ᴀ, ᴦó5ᴨᴀᴅ, to warn.

ᴅo or ᴀ, ᴨulᴀn5, to suffer.

ᴅo or ᴀ, 5ᴀƀáil, to take.

ᴅo or ᴀ, 5uíᴅe, to pray.

ᴅo or ᴀ, ṁᴀᴨċᴀin, to live.

ᴅo or ᴀ, ᴘóᴦᴀᴅ, to marry

ᴅo or ᴀ, ᴦeᴀċnᴀᴅ, to shun.

ᴅo or ᴀ, ᴨúƀᴀl, to walk.

ᴅo or ᴀ, ċᴀƀᴀiᴨċ, to give.

EXERCISE XVIII.

ᴅoᴨᴀᴦ, a door.

5o mᴀiċ, well.

5o cᴨom, heavily.

peᴀcᴀᴅ, sin.

ᴦ5ᴨioᴦ, ravage.

coil, will.

1. ƀuíᴅeᴀċᴀᴦ ᴅo ċᴀƀᴀiᴨċ. 2. ᴅo ċoil ᴀ ᴅeunᴀᴅ. 3. Seᴀn-ᴦeᴀᴨ ᴀ ᴘóᴦᴀᴅ. 4. Ⴀn mᴀᴅᴀᴅ ᴀ ċuᴘ ᴀmᴀċ. 5. Ⴀn ċiᴨ ᴅo[1] ᴦ5ᴨioᴦ. 6. Peᴀcᴀᴅ ᴀ ᴦeᴀcnᴀᴅ. 7. Ⴀn 5ᴀᴅuiᴅe ᴀ 5ᴀƀáil

[1] The learner will remember the rules about ᴦ in Exercise III., Section I.

8. An ꝼeaꝛ a ḃualaḋ ꝟo' cꝛom. 9. Pian a ꝼulanꝟ. 10. An ꝟoꝛaꝛ a ḋúnaḋ.

---

1. To give thanks. 2. Thy will to do. 3. To marry an old man. 4. To put out the dog. 5. To ravage the country. 6. To shun sin. 7. To take the thief. 8. To strike the man heavily. 9. To suffer pain. 10. To shut the door.

RULE IX.

Verbs beginning with a mutable consonant are aspirated in the perfect tense, indicative mood, active voice, and in the conditional mood of both voices. The particle ꝟo is generally placed before the verb in such instances; ꝛo is also used chiefly in composition with other particles as in ꝟuꝛ, ná'ꝛ, &c.

EXERCISE XIX.

Examples of ꝟo.

ꝟo ḃiḋeaꝛ, I was.

ꝟo ḃí mé, I was.

ꝟo ḃioꝟaꝛ, they were.

ꝟo ḃuailꝼinn, I would strike.

ꝟo ceannuiꝟ ꝛiḃ, ye bought.

ꝟo ḋún ꝛé, he shut.

ꝟ' ꝼóꝟluim ꝛé, he learned.

ꝟo ꝟꝛáḋuiꝟ ꝛé, he loved.

¹ The learner will remember that ꝟo before an adjective forms an adverb. See observations at foot of Exercise XIV., *First Book.*

ᴅo ṁaıṫ ṙé, he forgave.
ᴅo póᵹ ṙé, he kissed.
ᴅo ṡiúḃalṙainn, I would walk.
ᴅo ṫanᵹaᴅaṙ, they came.
ᴅo ṫiocṙá, thou wouldst come.
ᴅo ṫuᵹ ṙé, he gave.

EXERCISE XX.

aıṙᵹıoᴅ, silver, money. leaṫ, with thee.
ᴅóıḃ, to them. ṫú, thee.

1. ᴅo póᵹ ṙé é. 2. ᴅo ṁaıṫ ṙé ᴅóıḃ·
3. ᴅo ṫanᵹaᴅaṙ annṙın. 4. Ṡiúḃalṙainn
leaṫ. 5. Ṫuᵹ ṙé aıṙᵹıoᴅ ᴅóıḃ. 6. ᴅo ṫiocṙá
annṙo. 7. ᴅo ᵹṙáᴅuıᵹ ṙé a ṫíṙ. 8. ᴅ' ṙoᵹ
luım ṙé ᵹaeᴅılᵹe. 9. ᴅo ċeannuıᵹ ṙıḃ
leaḃaṙ. 10. ᴅo ḃuaılṙınn ṫú.

---

1. He kissed him. 2. He forgave (to) them.
3. They came there. 4. I would walk with
thee. 5. He gave money to them. 6. Thou
wouldst come here. 7. He loved his country.
8. He learned Irish. 9. Ye bought a book
10. I would strike thee.

Obs.—When the pronoun is expressed as in the above
instance, ᴅo ḃí mé, and in all the Examples hitherto used ir
these books, the verb is in the analytic form of conjugatior
and does not change in person or number. When the pro
noun is not expressed, but is included in the form of a verb,
as in the above instance, ᴅo ṫanᵹaᴅaṙ, the verb is in the
synthetic form, and changes in person and number. This
remark is made here to account for the verbs hitherto used
not having changed in person or number.

The sign ᴠo is often omitted, as in some of the above Examples. τú (τ dotted) is the accusative case of τú (thou); é of ᵳé, he ; ınn of ᵳınn, we ; ıb of ᵳıb, you ; ıaᴠ of ᵳıaᴠ, they. These forms are often used as nominatives with the verb ıᵳ. See Obs., page 17, *First Book.*

EXERCISE XXI.

Examples of ᵳo.

Ꝛo enters into the composition of the follow-ing particles which precede the perfect tense of verbs. It causes aspiration of the initial following it.

aᵳ, whether (in past time), compounded of an and ᵳo.

ᵹuᵳ, that (in past time), compounded of ᵹo and ᵳo.

munaᵳ, unless (in past time), compounded of muna and ᵳo.

ná'ᵳ—naᵹaᵳ, which not—that not (in time past), compounded of naᵹ and ᵳo.

naᵹaᵳ (interrogative), naᵹ and aᵳ, did not, whether not.

níoᵳ, not (in past time) compounded of ní and ᵳo.

aᵳ buaıl mé (whether) struck I.

ᵹuᵳ buaıl τú, that you struck.

munaᵳ buaıl ᵳé, if he did not strike (unless he struck).

naᵹaᵳ buaıl ᵳınn } that we did not strike.

ná'ᵳ buaılıᴅ ᵳınn } that we may not strike.

EXERCISE XXII.

ᴀn ᴄé, he who.   ḟoıllr̄ıᵹeᴀr, l showed.
beᴀnnuıᵹ, bless.   rcuıp, cease.
buᴀıleᴀr, I struck.   ċᴀınıc, came.

1. Ap buᴀıleᴀr?   2. Nıop ċᴀınıc ré.
3. Munᴀp ḟoıllr̄ıᵹeᴀr.   4. Ap buᴀıl ᴄú é ?
5. Nıop beᴀnnuıᵹ ᴄú mé.   6. Nıop rcuıp rınn.
7. An ᴅopᴀr nᴀċᴀp ɓún mé.   8. Leᴀbᴀp
nᴀċᴀp ᴄuᵹ ré.   9. An ᴄé nᴀċᴀp ᵹrᴀɓuıᵹ mé.
10. Nᴀ'p ċuıprɓ ré ríor é.

---

1. Did I strike? 2. He came not. 3. If I
have not shown. 4. Did you strike him ?
5. You did not bless me. 6. We did not cease.
7. The door which I did not shut. 8. A book
which he did not give. 9. He whom (the individual) I did not love. 10. That he may
not put it down.

RULE X.

Verbs beginning with a mutable consonant
are aspirated after ní, no, not ; má, if ; mᴀp,
as ; rul, before ; and after the relative pronoun ᴀ, who, which (sometimes ᴅo), whether
expressed or understood.

NOTE.—The relative pronoun ᴀ causes eclipsis (see page
63) when a preposition goes before it, but in the perfect tense
the participle no is joined to it, and aspiration takes place
(even with a preposition), except in some irregular verbs.
(See Rule 5, Eclipsis, page 62).

Exercise XXIII.

Examples.

ní béιὀ ré, he will not be.

ὁ ċαιlleαr é, who loses it.

ὁ ὀeunαr é, who does it.

mαr ḟoιllrιġeαnn mé, as I show.

ní ḟuιl ré, he is not.

ὁ ġráὀuιġ ιnn,[1] who loved us.

ὁ ṁeαllαr ιb,[1] who deceives you.

má pórαnn τú, if you marry.

má ḟαoιleαnn τú, if you think.

ὁ ḟαoιl, who thought.

rul ċαnζαr, before I came.

Exercise XXIV.

ὡ, nιs, ner, ιιs.   mαr rιn, so, as that.

1. Ní béιὀ ré ζο bráċ. 2. Αn τé ὁ ċαιlleαr αn cαċ. 3. Má ḟαoιleαnn τú mαr rιn. 4. Ιr é rιn ṁeαlαr mé. 5. Αn τé ὀo ġráὀuιġ ιnn.[1] 6. Ní ḟuιl ré αnn ro αnoιr. 7. Ιr é neαrτ ὁ ὀeunαr ceαrτ. 8. Má pórαnn τú reαnὀuιne. 9. Α ċαιll ὁ ḟláιnτe. 10. Mαr ḟoιllrιġeαr rul ċαnζαr.

---

1. It will not be for ever. 2. He who loses the battle. 3. If you think so. 4. It is that

[1] In the spoken language rιnn and rιb are more frequently used, but the forms ιnn and ιb are more correct in this case.

(which) deceives me.   5. The individual who loved us.   6. He is not here now.   7. It is might which makes right.   8. If you marry an old man.   9. Who lost his health.   10. As I showed before I came.

Obs.—Oo is frequently used before the perfect tense with the force of a relative pronoun, but ᴀ is also written before it, as in Examples above.

The learner should distinguish between the following words :—oo, thy (a possessive pronoun), oo, used as a rela-tive, oo, to (sign of infinitive), oo, particle before certain tenses), oo, to (prep.), oó, two, oó (prefix), oó, to him (prepositional pronoun).

And between these :—ᴀ, his, her, or their (possessive pro-noun), ᴀ, who, which (relative), ᴀ, to (sign of infinitive), ᴀ, o (sign of vocative case), ᴀ, ı, in (prep.)

These will be distinguished by their position and the context.

RULE XI.

The particles ᴀn, very; ꞟó, too, exceedingly; ꞟáꞟ, very, excessively, which are chiefly used as prefixes to adjectives, cause aspiration.

There are many particles, such as ᴀn, cor-responding to *in* or *un*, ᴀċ, corresponding to *re*, neᴀṁ. to *in* or *un*, &c., which cause aspiration ; but as these may be considered as forming compounds in each case with the word they precede, it is not necessary to give much attention to them here.

EXERCISE XXV.

Examples.

ⱥn-ḃpeⱥ̇ẋ, very fine.
ⱥn-ṁⱥ1ṫ, very good.
ⱥn-ṫó̇ẋ, misery; ⱥn (negative, *un*), and ṫó̇ẋ, happiness.
ⱥṫ-ḃeoṁu1ẋ, revive; ⱥṫ (*re*), and beoṁu1ẋ, animate.
ṽó-ḃeuⱤⱥ̇, ill-mannered.
ṽoċⱥṗ, loss, harm.
ṽó-ȯeunⱦⱥ (hard to be done), impossible.
ṽó-ḟe1ⱦ1onⱥ̇ (hard to be seen), invisible.
neⱥṁ-ⱦⱤóⱦⱥ1Ɽeⱥ̇, unmerciful.
Ɽó-ḃeⱥẋ, exceedingly small.
Ɽó-ṁóⱤ, too large.
Ɽó-ḟeⱥn, very old, too old.
Ɽó-ⱦe1ṫ, too hot.
ⱤⱥⱤ-ḃ1nn, most harmonious.
ⱤⱥⱤ-ẋⱡ1c, very wise.
ⱤⱥⱤ-ṁⱥ1ṫ, excellent.
Ɽó-ḃeuⱤⱥ̇, well-mannered.
ⱤóċⱥⱤ, profit.
Ɽó-ȯeunⱦⱥ (easy to be done), possible.
Ɽó-ḟe1ⱦ1onⱥ̇ (easy to be seen), visible.

NOTE.—An ı is generally inserted in spelling these prefixes, when the first vowel of the word following is slender. This shall be explained in its proper place, but for the present the attention of the learner need not be given to it.

50

ASPIRATION.

Exercise XXVI.

bᴀᵽeuᴅ, a hat
céᵽᴅ, a trade.
céᵽᴅe, of a trade.
ıon-ᴅeunᴄᴀ, fit to be done, practicable
ᵽᴀᵽuᵹᴀᴅ, oppression, fatigue.
ᵽeınn, sing.

1. Ꝺı ᵽé ᴀn-ꝺᵽeᴀᵹ. 2. Ꝺı ᴀ bᴀᵽeuᴅ ᵽó-
beᴀᵹ ᴅó. 3. Soċᴀᵽ ᴀᵹuᵽ ᴅoċᴀᵽ nᴀ céᵽᴅe.
4. Só-ᵽeıcᵽıonᴀċ ᴀᵹuᵽ ᴅó-ᵽeıcᵽıonᴀċ. 5. Ꞇᴀ
ᵽé ᵽó-ᴅeunᴄᴀ ᴀᵹuᵽ ıon-ᴅeunᴄᴀ. 6. Aᴄbeo·
ᴅuıᵹ ᴀn ᵹᴀeᴅılᵹe. 7. Sóᵹ ᴀᵹuᵽ ᴀn-ᵽóᵹ
8. An-ᵽóᵹ ᴀᵹuᵽ ᵽᴀᵽuᵹᴀᴅ. 9. Ꝺo ᵽeınn ᵽı ᵹo
ᵽᴀᵽ-bınn. 10. Iᵽ ᵽᴀᵽ-ṁᴀıᴄ ᴀn ᵽeᴀᵽ é.

---

1. It was very fine. 2. His hat was too
small for him. 3. (The) profit and loss of the
trade. 4. Visible and invisible. 5. It is possible and practicable. 6. Revive the Gaelic.
7. Happiness and misery. 8. Misery and
oppression. 9. She sang most harmoniously.
10. He is an excellent man.

Obs.—Só and ᴅó are here used; ᴅó is the opposite of ᵽó.
They are used before nouns, adjectives, and participles,
and sometimes are entirely incorporated in the word.
Before nouns and adjectives ᴅó equals *ill*, ᵽó the opposite.
Before participles ᴅó implies difficulty; ᵽó, easɢᴀ· ıon,
fitness.

RULE XII.

(*a.*) The prepositions ᴀıṗ, on ; ᴅe, of. or off ; ᴅo, to ; ꝼᴀoı or ꝼᴀ, under ; ıᴅıṗ, between ; mᴀṗ, like to, as ; ó, from ; ꜩᴀṗ, over ; ꜩṗe, through ; um, about, cause aspiration of the initial of all nouns following them (if aspirable). The adjective accompanying a feminine noun in such case is aspirated.

(*b.*) When the article accompanies a noun, the preposition going before generally causes eclipsis of the initial of the noun in the singular number, except ᴅe and ᴅo, which in such case cause aspiration.

EXERCISE XXVII.

Examples.

ᴀıṗ ṁullᴀċ, on top, at the summit.

ᴅe ḃᴀṗṗ, from top or head.

ᴅe ḃṗıᵹ, because.

ᴅo ċoṗp, to a body.

ᴅo Ḋıᴀ, to God.

ꝼᴀoı ṁeᴀṗ, in (literally "under") esteem.

ꝼᴀ ċuᴀıṗım,[1] in the direction of.

ıᴅıṗ ꝼeᴀṗᴀıḃ, among men.

mᴀṗ ᵹeᴀll, as a promise, because.

mᴀṗ ṁᴀᵹᴀḋ, like to, or as mocking.

ó ċṗᴀnn, from a tree.

ó ꝼeᴀṗ, from a man.

ꜩᴀṗ ṗuꞇ, over a lip.

ꜩṗe ċeıne (through), on fire.

[1] ꝼᴀ ċuᴀıṗım is used idiomatically for *towards*, oꝛ *in the direction of;* ꞇuᴀıṗım means a *guess,* or *conjecture.*

Obs.—There are a few exceptions to above Rule, which occur for the most part in adverbial expressions; as, ᴀιꞃ mᴀιᴅιn, in the morning; ó ꞃo ᴀmᴀċ, from this out ; ᴀιꞃ bᴀll, on the spot, immediately.

Ꙅᴀn, without, will have either primary or aspirated form, according to the taste of the speaker. Ꙗꙅ, ᴀꞃ, ꙅo, le, óꞃ, do not cause aspiration.

A few simple prepositions eclipse, as shown, page 62.

EXERCISE XXVIII.

béιᴅ, will be.	mnᴀιb (*dat. pl.*) women.
boċc, poor.	ꞃeᴀmꞃóꙅ, a shamrock.
cꞃᴀιnn, of a tree.	ꞃláιnce, health.
lᴀbꞃᴀnn (*hab.*) speaks	cιꙅe, of a house.

1. 'O cꞃᴀnn ꙅo¹ cꞃᴀnn. 2. ᴌᴑιꞃ ꝼeᴀꞃᴀιb ᴀꙅuꞃ mnᴀιb. 3. Ꙗιꞃ mᴀιᴅιn bꞃeᴀꙅ. 4. 'O ꝼeᴀꞃ boċc. 5. ᴅe bꞃιꙅ ꙅo lᴀbꞃᴀnn ꞃé. 6. Cuιꞃ ꞃeᴀmꞃóꙅ ᴀnn ᴅo bᴀιꞃeuᴅ. 7. Ꝼᴀ ċuᴀιꞃιm ᴅo ꝼláιnce. 8. béιᴅ ᴀn ꙅᴀeᴅιlꙅe ꞃᴀoι meᴀꞃ ꝼóꞃ. 9. ᴅe bᴀꞃꞃ ᴀn cꞃᴀιnn. 10. Ꙗιꞃ mullᴀċ ᴀn cιꙅe.

---

1. From tree to tree. 2. Between men and women. 3. On a fine morning. 4. From a poor man. 5. Because (that) he speaks. 6. Put a shamrock in your hat. 7. Towards your health. 8. The Gaelic will be yet in esteem. 9. From the top of the tree. 10. On the top of the house.

---

¹ See observations on Rule XII. for exceptions.

EXERCISE XXIX.

On ᴠe, ᴠo, ʒᴀn, and ιᴠιρ.

mᴀρᴮ, dead.

mnᴀoι, *dat.* of bean, a woman.

1. Ꝺo'n[1] ċoρρ mᴀρᴮ.   2. Ꝺo'n ᴮᴀιle móρ.
3. Ꝺo'n ᴠoρᴀρ[2].   4. Ꝺo'n[2] Ċιʒeᴀρnᴀ.   5. ʒᴀn
ᴀn ceιne.   6. ʒᴀn ᴀn[3] ρeᴀρ.   7. ιᴠιρ ᴀn[3] cρᴀnn
ᴀʒυρ ᴀn ceιne.   8. Ꝺo'n ṁυllᴀċ ᴀρᴠ.   9. Ꝺe'n
ᴮᴀρρ.   10. ιᴠιρ ᴀn ρeᴀρ ᴀʒυρ ᴀn ᴮeᴀn.

1. To the dead body.   2. To the large town.
3. To the door.   4. To the Lord.   5. Without
the fire.   6. Without the man.   7. Between
the tree and the fire.   8. To the lofty summit.
9. Off the top.   10. Between the man and the
woman.

RULE XIII.

The interjection ᴀ, sign of the *vocative* case,
always causes aspiration both in singular and
plural of nouns and singular number of adjectives.

[1] The ᴀ of the article is left out after the vowel of the preposition.

[2] See observations on Rule I. concerning nouns with ᴠ or
c.   Nouns beginning with ρ are eclipsed.

[3] ʒᴀn, with or without the article, causes no change in the
initials of nouns.   ιᴠιρ causes no change in the singular
number.

Exercise XXX.

ᴀ ḃeᴀn, O woman.

ᴀ ċlᴀ-ḋᴀıᵱe, O coward.

ᴀ ḋᴀoıne, O people.

ᴀ ḋeᴀᵱḃᵱáċᴀıᵱ, O brother.

ᴀ 'Ḋıᴀ ṁóıᵱ, O Great God.

ᴀ ḋuıne ḋonᴀ, O unfortunate man.

ᴀ ᵱıᵱ, O man.

ᴀ ᵹᵱáḋ, O love.

ᴀ ṁná, O women.

χᴀ ṁuıᵱe öılıᵱ, O dear Mary.

ᴀ ᵱáıᵱḋe ḃıᵹ, O little child.

ᴀ ᵱeᴀnᵱıᵱ ᵱonᴀ, O fortunate old man.

ᴀ Ċıᵹeᴀᵱnᴀ, O Lord.

Exercise XXXI

cléıḃ, of a bosom.

clıᴀḃ, a bosom.

cóıᵱ, just.

ᵹıl (voc.), bright.

uᴀıᵱle, noble (plu. of uᴀᵱᴀl).

1. ᴀ ᵹᵱáḋ ᵹıl mo ċᵱoıḋe. 2. ᴀ ċᴀᵱᴀ öılıᵱ. 3. ᴀ ḋeᴀᵱḃᵱáċᴀıᵱ mo cléıḃ. 4. ᴀ ḋuıne cóıᵱ. 5. ᴀ ċuıᵱle mo ċᵱoıḋe. 6. ᴀ ᵱıᵱ ṁᴀıċ. 7. ᴀ ᵱeᴀn-ᵱıᵱ öılıᵱ. 8. ᴀ ṁná ᵱonᴀ. 9. ᴀ ḃeᴀn uᴀᵱᴀl[1] ṁᴀıċ, 10. ᴀ ḋᴀoıne uᴀıᵱle.[1]

___

1. O bright love of my heart. 2. O dear friend. 3. O brother of my bosom. 4. Honest

, ḃeᴀn uᴀᵱᴀl, a noble or gentle woman, a lady; ḋuıne ᴀᵱᴀl, a noble man, a gentleman. Plural, ḋᴀoıne vᴀıᵱle, and mná uᴀıᵱle.

man.   5. O pulse of my heart.   6. Good man.
7. O dear old man.   8. O fortunate women.
9. Good lady.   10. Gentlemen.

The foregoing Rules contain all the instances
in which there can be any grammatical neces-
sity for aspiration, and the learner has now
mastered in these thirteen Rules the most
difficult feature of the Irish language.

PART II.

ECLIPSIS.

In eclipsis the sound of certain initial consonants is changed in certain cases by the influence of the preceding word into that of a
kindred letter, which is more easily sounded
under the circumstances, and which, for the
sake of euphony, is substituted for it.   This
letter is now generally written before the letter
of which it eclipses or suppresses the sound,
and is separated from it by a hyphen, thus : ᴀ
m-báᴅ, *our boat*.   This system, though giving
the words something of a crowded appearance,
is to be preferred to that adopted by the Welsh
and Manx, who change the initial letter both
for aspiration and eclipsis, thus destroying the
radical initial of the word, and rendering it
unrecognisable.

The difficulty of eclipsis is entirely on the
surface, and the learner will soon notice that it

enables words in certain positions to be sounded more easily than if their initials were left in their radical state. Thus m after ɼ in ár máɔ, which is the sound of the phrase given above —ár m-báɔ—is more easily sounded than if the initial b had been retained, as ár báɔ. The sound of b is lost, but to remove the letter would lead to great confusion.

The following Rules contain the whole system of eclipsis as laid down by grammarians. Though, of course, based on euphony, eclipsis does not (like aspiration) take place in any instance in words uninfluenced by certain others, being governed either by rules of grammar, or by the position of the influenced word. All consonants can be eclipsed except the four liquids, l, m, n, and ɼ. The letters which are employed to eclipse others are b, ɔ, ʒ, m, n, c, and the aspirated ɓ.

Table of Eclipsed Letters.

m eclipses b, as ár m-báɔ, our boat, pronounced as if ár máɔ (*or mawdh*).

ʒ eclipses c, as ár ʒ-ceárc, our right, pronounced as if ár ʒeárc (*or garth*).

n eclipses ɔ, as ɓur n-ɔorár, your door, pronounced as if ɓur norur (*wur nurus*).

ɓ eclipses p, as ɓur ɓ-páirɔe, your child, pronounced as if ɓur báirɔe (*wur bawishthe*).

ɔ eclipses c, as á ɔ-cír, their country, pronounced as if á ɔír (*a dheer*).

ḃ eclipses ꝼ, as ᴀ ḃ-ꝼuil, their blood, pronounced as if ᴀ ḃuil (*a will*).

n eclipses ᵹ, as ᴀ nᵹᴀḃᴀꝺ, their goat, pronounced as if ᴀ nᵹᴀḃᴀꝺ.

ꞇ eclipses ꞅ, as ᴀn ꞇ-ꞅlᴀꞇ, the rod, pronounced as if ᴀn ꞇlᴀꞇ.

Here it is seen that the radical initial of each of the eight nouns given above takes the sound of the letter by which it is eclipsed, and which unites more harmoniously with the preceding consonant.

The last three instances shown above are peculiar. In the case of ꝼ eclipsed by ḃ we have an aspirate letter (equivalent to *v* or *w*) eclipsing a radical.

In the case of nᵹ, n does not, properly speaking, eclipse ᵹ, but the two letters form one sound (which has been shown in the *First Book*, note on Exercise XII.), and which, when initial is best learned from an Irish speaker. These letters are not separated by a hyphen.

The letter ꞅ is eclipsed by ꞇ, but only in nouns influenced by the article ᴀn. (See Rule VII).

RULE I.

Eclipsis takes place after the possessive pronouns ᴀꝛ, our ; ḃuꝺ, your ; ᴀ, their.

Exercise I.

bⱤⁱⱴⱪⱸ, broken.   ⱴóċⱥⱃ, hope.
cⱥⱃⱃⱥⁱⱬ, a rock.

1. Ⱥⱃ ⱴ-ⱦⱥⱡⱥ́ṁ. 2. Ḃⁱ ⱥ n-ⱴóċⱥⱃ ⱡⱥ́ⁱⱴⁱⱃ
3. Ⱦⱥ́ ḃuⱃ ḃ-pⱥ́ⁱⱃⱴe ⱦⁱnn. 4. Ⱳⁱ ⱶuⁱⱡ ḃuⱃ
ⱬ-cⱥⱃⱥ ⱥnn ⱃⱺ. 5. Ⱦⱥ́ ⱥ ḃ-ⱶeⱥⱃⱥnn ⱬⱡⱥⱃ.
6. Ḃⁱ ⱥ nⱬeⱥⱡⱡ cⁱnnⱦe. 7. Ⱦⱥ́ ⱥⱃ m-buⱥò-
ⱥⁱⱃⱦ ⱦⱃⱺm. 8. Ⱦⱥ́ ⱥⱃ 'ⱃⱡⱥ́ⁱnⱦe mⱥⁱⱦ. 9. Ⱦⱥ́
ⱥⱃ m-bⱥⱺ bⱤⁱⱴⱪⱸ ⱡe cⱥⱃⱃⱥⁱⱬ. 10. Ⱥ ⱴ-ⱦⁱⱃ
ⱥⱬuⱃ ⱥ muⁱnⱦⁱⱃ.

---

1. Our land. 2. Their hope was strong.
3. Your child is sick. 4. Your friend is not
here. 5. Their field is green. 6. Their promise was sure. 7. Our trouble is heavy.
8. Our health is good. 9. Our boat is broken
by a rock. 10. Their country and their
people

RULE II.

Eclipsis takes place in the genitive plural
of nouns when the article is expressed.

The adjective accompanying the noun in this case is sometimes eclipsed, but this is not necessary.

' Nouns beginning with ⱃ form an exception to above
Rules. (See Rule VII., page 65, for eclipsis of initial ⱃ).

Exercise II.

Examples.

na m-bád, of the boats.
na m-bárd, of the bards.
na m-beaċ, of the bees.
na m-bó, of the cows.
na g-cearc, of the hens.
na n-dán, of the poems.
na ḃ-fileaḋ, of the poets.
na ngeall, of the promises.
na ngort, of the fields
na b-páisdeaḋ, of the children.
na d-tonn, of the waves.

Exercise III.

bláṫ, a blossom.
cogar, a whisper.
fuaim, a sound.
mil, honey.
nós, a habit.
uḃ, an egg.
uiḃe, eggs.

1. Mil na m-beaċ. 2. Gort na m-bó
3. Bláṫ na ngort. 4. Flaiṫ na ḃ-fileaḋ.
5. Fuaim na d-tonn. 6. Nós na b-daisdeaḋ.
7. Uiḃe na g-cearc. 8. Cogar na sruṫ.
9. Bláṫ na g-crann. 10. Leaḃar na n-dán.

---

1. Honey of the bees.[1] 2. (The) field of the cows. 3. (The) blossom of the fields. 4. Prince of the poets. 5. (The) sound of the waves. 6. (The) habit of the children. 7. (The) eggs of the hens. 8. (The) whispering of the streams. 9. (The) blossom of the trees. 10. (The) book of the poems.

[1] See note, page 29.

RULE III.

The prepositions ᴀᴃ, at ; ᴀ⁊ꞃ, on ; ᴀnnꞃ (or ⁊ꞃ), in ; ᴀꞃ, out of; ꝼᴀо⁊ or ꝼᴀ, under ; ᴃuꞃ, towards; lе⁊ꞃ, with ; mᴀꞃ, like, as ; ó, from ; ᴄᴀꞃ, over; ᴄꞃе, ᴄꞃеᴀꞃ, through ; um, about; when followed by the article, cause eclipsis of the initials of nouns in the singular number only. The adjective is generally aspirated in such instances when qualifying a feminine noun.

EXERCISE IV.
Examples.

ᴀᴃ ᴀn m-bᴀ⁊n-ꝼé⁊ꞃ, at the wedding.
ᴀ⁊ꞃ ᴀn ᴅ-ᴄᴀlᴀ́ṁ, on the earth.
ᴀnnꞃ (or ⁊ꞃ) ᴀn ᴄ-ꞃᴀоᴃᴀl, in the world.
ᴀꞃ ᴀn ᴃ-cо⁊ꞃe, out of the cauldron.
ꝼᴀо⁊ ᴀn b-pé⁊n, under the pain.
ᴃuꞃ ᴀn m-bᴀ⁊le, to the town.
lе⁊ꞃ ᴀn ᴃ-clᴀ́⁊ṫeᴀ́ṁ, with the sword.
mᴀꞃ ᴀn ᴃ-ceuᴅnᴀ, as the same, likewise.
ó'n nᴃоꞃᴄ, from the field.
ᴄᴀꞃ ᴀn ᴃ-ꝼᴀ⁊ꞃᴃe, over the sea.
ᴄꞃe 'n or } ᴅоꞃᴀꞃ, through the door.
ᴄꞃeᴀꞃ ᴀn }
um ᴀn ᴄ-ꞃоluꞃ, about the light.

EXERCISE V.

cuṁᴀnᴃ, narrow.   m⁊ꞃe, I myself.
ꝼᴀ⁊ꞃꞃ⁊nᴃ, wide.

1. Bí ſé aᵹ an m-bain-ḟéiſ. 2. Aᵹuſ miſe maſ an ᵹ-ceuona. 3. Ní ḟuil ſé annſan m-baile. 4. Cuiſ annſ an ᵹ-coiſe é. 5. Do ċanᵹaoaſ⁊ ⱦe 'n oopaſ cuṁanᵹ. 6. Do buail ſé leiſ an ᵹ-cláiöeaṁ é. 7. Taſ an b-ſaiſᵹe ṁóiſ. 8. 'O'n nᵹoſⱦ ᵹlaſ. 9. Aſ an ⱦ-ſſáio ſaiſſinᵹ. 10. Suſ an ⱦ-ſoluſ.

---

1. He was at the wedding. 2. And myself likewise. 3. He is not in the town. 4. Put it in the cauldron. 5. They came through the narrow door. 6. He struck him with the sword. 7. Over the great sea. 8. From the green field. 9. Out of the wide street. 10. To the light.

OBS.—D, being eclipsed by n, takes no letter before it in Example 5, as the n of an, the article, is sufficiently euphonic. ⱦ is very often not eclipsed by o, when an goes before, as the union of n and ⱦ does not require eclipsis.

Annſ is a form of the preposition ann, which is used for euphony before the article an. Leiſ is used in the same way, and often before the relative pronoun a, instead of le, ᵹuſ instead of ᵹo, iſ istead of i or a, ⱦſeſ or ⱦſeaſ, instead of ⱦſe.

Prepositions ending in a vowel cause a of the article to be dropped as in the foregoing examples. See Exercise XXIX., page 53. See note, page 69, for some examples, where they precede other words begirning with vowels.

RULE IV.

The prepositions ᴀ or 1, *in*; 1ᴀᴘ, *after*; ᴘ1ᴀ, *before* (now obsolete), cause eclipsis with or without ᴀn.

Exercise VI.

bᴀ1ᴌe, a town (home).	ᴅuᴌ, going.
cé1n, ⎫ distant.	ᴘoᴣuᴘ, near.
c1ᴀn, ⎭	ᴘ1ᴀᴅ-ᴘo, these.
ᴅᴀ1ᴌ, a meeting.	ᴘ1ᴀᴅ-ᴘ1n, those.
ᴅ1bᴘeᴀᴅ, exile.	ᴄeᴀᴄᴄ, coming.

1. Ꭺ m-bᴀ1ᴌe. 2. Ꭺ n-ᴅ1bᴘeᴀᴅ. 3. 1ᴀᴘ n-ᴅuᴌ. 4. Ꭾ1 ᴘ1ᴀᴅ-ᴘo ᴀ m-bᴀ1ᴌe. 5. Ꭾ1 ᴘ1ᴀᴅ-ᴘ1n ᴀ n-ᴅ1bᴘeᴀᴅ. 6. Ꭺ ᴃ-ᴘoᴣuᴘ no ᴀ ᴣ-céin. 7. 1ᴀᴘ ᴅ-ᴄeᴀᴄᴄ. 8. Ꭺ ᴘᴌᴀ1nᴄe ᴍᴀ1ᴄ. 9. 1ᴀᴘ ᴅ-ᴄeᴀᴄᴄ Ᵽᴀᴅᴘᴀ1c. 10. 1ᴘ' ᴀn ᴅᴀ1ᴌ.

---

1. At home (in town). 2. In exile. 3. After going. 4. These were at home. 5. Those were in exile. 6. Near or far. 7. After coming. 8. In good health. 9. After the coming of Patrick. 10. In the meeting.

Obs.—Ꭺ m-bᴀ1ᴌe or ᴘᴀ m-bᴀ1ᴌe is used for *at home.*

RULE V.

The particles ᴀn, whether; ᴣo, that;[2] nᴀċ, that not; ᴅᴀ, if; cᴀ, where; munᴀ, unless, if not; cause eclipsis in verbs, as also the relative

[1] See observations, page 61.
[2] ᴣo, when prefixed to an adjective to form an adverb, does not aspirate or eclipse. (Obs. on Exercise XᴛV., *First Book.*)

ᴀ, who, or which, when preceded by a preposition expressed or understood, and when signifying "all which" or "all that."

EXERCISE VII.

áιτ, a place.	ρeιceᴀnn, sees.
béᴀρρᴀ𝑖, would give.	ρoιllριʒeᴀnn, shows.
buᴀιleᴀnn, strikes.	b-ρuιl, is.
cιᴀnnoρ, how.	b-ρuιlιm, I am, am I?
oeᴀċᴀι𝑖, went.	τéι𝑖, go.

1. ᴀn m-buᴀιleᴀnn ρé? 2. ʒo 𝑖-τéι𝑖 τú ρlán. 3. ɴᴀċ b-ρeιceᴀnn τú? 4. ɱunᴀ b-ρoιllριʒeᴀnn ρé é. 5. 'Αιτ ᴀnn ᴀ b-ρuιlιm. 6. Cá b-ρuιl Pᴀ𝑖ρᴀιc? 7. 𝑂á m-béᴀρρᴀ𝑖 ρé míle bó 𝑖ᴀm. 8. Cá n-𝑖eᴀċᴀι𝑖 τú? 9. ᴀn b-ρuιl τú ʒo mᴀιτ? 10. Tá mé ʒo mᴀιτ; cιᴀnnoρ ᴀ b-ρuιl τú ρéιn?

1. Does he strike? 2. That you may go safe. 3. Do you not see? 4. Unless he show it. 5. The place where (in which) I am. 6. Where is Patrick? 7. If he should give 'to) me a thousand cows. 8. Where did you go? 9. (Whether) are you well? 10. I ar: well ; how are you yourself?

OBS.—The forms of these particles used with the perfect tense (ᴀρ, &c.) have already been shown in Rules for Aspiration, Exercise XXI.

The relative pronoun ᴀ, who, which, when used with the perfect tense becomes ᴀρ', and, even though preceded by a preposition, aspirates the following initial of verbs by the influence of ρo, which is joined to it except in irregular verbs. (See page 46.)

RULE VI.

The *Cardinal* numbers ꞃeáċꞇ, seven ; oċꞇ, eight ; naoı, nine ; and ꝺeıċ, ten, cause eclipsis of nouns following them, except when the noun begins with ꞃ.

Ꝺá eclipses in Ꝺá ꝺ-ꞇꞃıan, two-thirds.

EXERCISE VIII.

am, time.	luaċ, price.
aoıꞃ. age.	mıoꞃa, months.
beannaċꞇ, a blessing.	pıȝın, a penny.
cıll, a church.	pıȝne, pence.
cláꞃ, a table.	ꞃaȝaıꞃꞇ, priests.
ȝeıneálaıȝe, genera- tions.	ꞃaoıꞃ, carpenters.

1. Seáċꞇ m-blıaóna. 2. Ꝺı ꞃé oċꞇ m-blıaóna ꝺeuȝ ꝺ' aoıꞃ. 3. Ꝺı oċꞇ ȝ-coꞃa aȝ an ȝ-cláꞃ. 4. Iꞃ é a luaċ naoı b-pıȝne. 5. Ꝺı ꝺeıċ n-ꝺaoıne ann ꞃın. 6. Ꝺı ꝺeıċ ꞃaoıꞃ aȝ an obaıꞃ. 7. Ꝺı ꞃeáċꞇ mıoꞃa ó 'n am ꞃın. 8. Ꝺı ꝺeıċ ꞃaȝaıꞃꞇ annꞃ an ȝ-cıll. 9. Seáċꞇ mıle beannaċꞇ oꞃꞇ. 10. Oċꞇ nȝeıneálaıȝe.

---

1. Seven years. 2. He was eighteen years of age. 3. (There) were eight feet to the table. 4. Its price is nine pence. 5. There were ten persons there. 6. (There) were ten carpenters at the work. 7. There were seven

months since that time. 8. Ten priests were in the church 9. Seven thousand blessings on you. 10. Eight generations.

The numbers which aspirate have been already treated of (page 39).

RULE VII.

OF ᚆ BEFORE ᚏ.

Nouns beginning with ᚏ are eclipsed by ᚆ, when the article is expressed, as follows :

1. Feminine nouns in the nominative, accusative, and dative singular.

2. Masculine nouns in the genitive and dative singular.

Nouns beginning with ᚏ are most generally eclipsed in the dative case, only after the prepositions ᚃᚓ, ᚃᚑ, and ᚐᚅᚅᚏ or ᚔᚏ.

EXERCISE IX.

Examples of feminine nouns (nominative and accusative).

ᚐᚅ ᚆ-ᚏᚐᛁᛚ, the beam.   ᚐᚅ ᚆ-ᚏᚉᚑ́ᚅ, the nose.
ᚐᚅ ᚆ-ᚏᛚᚐᚆ, the rod.   ᚐᚅ ᚆ-ᚏᚒᛁᛚ, the eye.

Examples of masculine nouns (genitive).

ᚐᚅ ᚆ-ᚏᚐᚷᚐᛁᚏᚆ, of the priest.
ᚐᚅ ᚆ-ᚏᚐᚅᚷᚐᛁᛚ, of the world.
ᚐᚅ ᚆ-ᚏᚓᚑᛁᛚ, of the sail.
ᚐᚅ ᚆ-ᚏᚒᛁᚃᚓ, of the session.

Examples of both genders (dative)

ᴅo'n c-ᴘᴀ5ᴀᴘc (*m.*), to the priest.
ó'n c-ᴘᴀo5ᴀl (*m.*), from the world.
ᴀᴘ ᴀn c-ᴘeol (*m.*), on the sail.
ᴅo'n c-ᴘlᴀ1c (*f.*), to the rod.
ᴀnnᴘ ᴀn c-ᴘúil (*f.*) in the eye.
ᴀ5 ᴀn c-ᴘᴘóin (*f.*) at the nose.

S, followed by b, c, ᴅ, 5, m, p, c, can neithei be eclipsed nor aspirated, as before showr. (page 22) ; the reason is that c, followed by these letters (ᴘ of course being suppressed), could not be pronounced, neither could ᴘ̇ (dotted) be pronounced before these letters.

ᴀn ᴘ5ᴀn (*f.*), the knife.
ᴅo'n ᴘcᴀċ (*m.*), to the shadow.
ᴀᴘ ᴀn ᴘcᴀ1ċ (*f.*), on the shield.
lᴇᴘ ᴀn ᴘooc (*m.*), with the trumpet.
ó'n ᴘmᴘoᴘ (*m.*), from the marrow.
ᴀn ᴘᴘᴀ1lᴘin (*m.*), of the labourer.

OBS.—Examples of ᴘ eclipsed by c in the dative have beec already given under Rule III., on the preposition with the article. The preposition is always used with the dative.

The rule does not apply in any case of the plural. S here may be said to follow the rules of aspiration rather than eclipsis as regards the instances in which the change of sound takes place; but after ᴅe and ᴅo, &c., with the article it is eclipsed, as with the other prepositions.

Exercise X.

ſaᴅ, far.	ſeoᴅ, a jewel.
lean, follow.	ſuíᴅeacán, a seat.
méiᴅ, size.	ceac, a house.
ſéiᴅ, blow.	cabaiſ, give.

1. Ceac an c-ſaꜱaiſc. 2. Seoᴅ an c-ſao-ꜱail. 3. Méiᴅ an c-ſeoil. 4. Fuaim an ſooic. 5. ᴅo buail ſé an c-ſail (*acc. fem.*). 6. Cabaiſ an ſuíᴅeacán (*acc. mas.*) ᴅo'n c-ſa-ꜱaſc. 7. Cóꜱ aſ an c-ſúil é. 8. A b-ſaᴅ ó'n c-ſaoꜱal. 9 Lean é aiſ an c-ſſáiᴅ. 10. ᴅo ſéiᴅ ſé leiſ an ſooc.

---

1. (The) house of the priest. 2. (The) jewel of the world. 3. (The) size of the sail. 4. (The) sound of the trumpet. 6. He struck the beam. 6. Give the seat to the priest. 7. Take it out of the eye. 8. Far from the world. 9. Follow him on the street. 10. He blew with the trumpet.

Of the use of n, c, *and* h, *before nouns beginning with vowels.*

The rules regarding this peculiar use of c and n, and the aspirate h, do not, strictly speaking, come under the head of Eclipsis, because a vowel cannot be eclipsed ; but in order not to multiply grammatical terms, we treat of them here.

RULE VIII.

n BEFORE VOWELS.

In every instance where an initial *consonant* would be eclipsed, words beginning with a vowel will take an n before them, except where an is expressed; the n of an is then sufficient.

Exfrcise XI.—Examples.

Under Rule I.

ar n-arán, our bread. ḃur n-obair, your work.
ar n-aṫair, our father. a n-euḋaċ, their clothes.

Under Rule II.

na n-anfa, of the storms.
na n-eun, of the birds.
na n-iasg, of the fish.
na n-óiġ, of the virgins.
na n-uḃ, of the eggs.

Under Rule IV.

a n-ainm, in name. iar n-ól, after drinking
i n-Éirinn, in Ireland. a n-uaṫḃár, in terror.
a n-olainn, in wool.

Under Rule V.

go n-inneosad, that I will tell.
naċ n-eitillim, do I not fly?
dá n-ólfainn, if I should drink.

Under Rule VI.

ſeaċċ n-aḃɼáin, seven songs.
oċċ n-eiċ, eight steeds.
naoi n-oiɼʋ, nine sledges.
ʋeiċ n-inġeana, ten daughters.

EXERCISE XII.

ʋuinn, to us.   eiċleaʋ, flight.

1. A n-ainm an Aċaɼ.   2. Aɼ n-Aċaiɼ.
3. Taḃaiɼ aɼ n-aɼán ʋuinn.   4. Iaɼ ʋ-ċeaċċ
Ṗáoɼaic i n-Éiɼinn.   5. Beannaċċ aiɼ ṫuɼ
n-obaiɼ.   6. Ḃí ɼé a n-uaċḃáɼ.   7. Ḃí ɼeaċċ
n-aḃɼáin annɼ an Leaḃaɼ.   8. Ḃí ʋeiċ n-inġeana aiġe.   9. Eiċleaʋ na n-eun.   10. ʋá
n-ólɼainn uiɼġe ɼuaɼ.

---

1. In (the) name of the Father.   2. Oui
Father.   3. Give (to) us our bread.   4. Aftei
(the) coming of Patrick to Ireland.   5. A
blessing on your work.   6. He was in terror.
7. (There) were seven songs in the book,
8. (There) were ten daughters with him (he
had, &c.).   9. (The) flight of the birds.   10. If
I should drink cold water.

Obs.—n is often inserted for euphony between preposi‑
tions ending in a vowel, and the relative and possessive pro‑
nouns a coming after, as Lé n-a ɼúil, with her eye ; ó n-a ḃ‑
ɼuil, from which is &c.   See page 71.

5

RULE IX.

ᴄ BEFORE VOWELS.

All *masculine* nouns beginning with vowels take ᴄ prefixed in the nominative and accusative case *singular*, when the article ᴀn is expressed.

EXERCISE XIII.

ᴀnᴀm, a soul.   múrᵹᴀil, awaken.
mᴀrḃ, kill.

1. An ᴄ-ᴀnᴀm. 2. An ᴄ-eun ᴀᵹur ᴀn ᴄ-iᴀrᵹ. 3. An ᴄ-uirᵹe ꝼuᴀr. 4. buᴀil ᴀn ᴄ-uirᵹe. 5. Múrᵹᴀil ᴀn ᴄ-ᴀnᴀm. 6. Mᴀrḃ ᴀn ᴄ-eun. 7. Ḃi ᴀn ᴄ-eᴀċ lᴀiᴅir. 8. ᴅo ꝼeinn ré ᴀn ᴄ-ᴀḃrᴀn. 9. An ᴄ-ᴀnᴀm ᴀᵹur ᴀn ċolᴀnn. 10. ᵹlᴀc ᴀn ᴄ-ᴀrᴀn.

---

1. The soul. 2. The bird and the fish. 3. The cold water. 4. Strike the water (*acc.*). 5. Awaken the soul (*acc.*). 6. Kill the bird. 7. The steed was strong. 8. He sang the song. 9. The soul and the body. 10. Take the bread.

OBS.— *Feminine* nouns beginning with a vowel never take a ᴄ, as its use is principally to distinguish gender.

RULE X.

USE OF h.

Nouns beginning with a vowel take h prefixed to prevent a hiatus, when the article na is expressed (except in the genitive plural, which takes n). h is also placed after the possessive pronoun, a, *her*, when the word following begins with a vowel.

The use of h prefixed to words beginning with vowels hardly comes under rules of grammar, as it is entirely regulated by euphony, and a desire to prevent a hiatus between two vowels, as Le h-Iosa, *with Jesus*. The instances given in the above rule are the only occasions when h answers any grammatical purpose.

Obs.—A (possessive pronoun) *his*, aspirates initial letters if aspirable; if not, no change takes place, even when a vowel follows. A, *her*, does not change the initial consonant in any case, but takes h before a vowel as above. A, *their*, eclipses the initial (if eclipsable), and prefixes n if the following word begins with a vowel. See Exercise II., Rule VIII., and XV., Rule VII., Part I.

Exercise XIV.

aḋarca, horns. inse (*gen.*) of an island.
aille (*gen.*), of a cliff. Líon, fill.
áilleaċt, beauty. na, of the.
baois, folly. ocras, hunger.

1. Na h-aḋarca. 2. Bárr na h-aille. 3. Na h-inse. 4. A h-ainm. 5. A anam. 6. Baois

na h-óiʒe. 7. Oo lion ré é le h-uirʒe.
8. le ¹n-a h-áilleaċc. 9. O'a ocpar. 10. le
h-iarʒ aʒur le h-eun.

———

1. The horns. 2. (The) top of the cliff.
3. Of the island. 4. Her name. 5. His soul.
6. (The) folly of (the) youth. 7. He filled it with
water. 8. With her beauty. 9. To (or of) his
hunger. 10. With a fish and with a bird.

———

Ċa, not (probably a form of noċa, now obsolete), is used in Ulster and in Scotland for
ní. It requires n to be prefixed to words beginning with a vowel or r; as ċa n-ḟuil ré, he
is not, for ní ḟuil ré, or ní b-ḟuil ré. buċ or
ba the perfect tense of the assertive verb ir,
often aspirates the initial of the succeeding
word, as, buð ṁaiċ é, he was good.

A few instances of aspiration and eclipsis
occurring under conditions different from any
laid down in the foregoing Rules, may be met
with in Irish books. Things so closely con-
nected with euphony and elegance of expres-
sion, as aspiration and eclipsis undoubtedly
are, cannot in all cases be reduced to precise
rules ; but those given are sufficient to explain
their use.

¹ See note page 69.

Short Phrases Illustrating foregoing Rules
VOCABULARY.

ᴀɪcɪ (at or) with her.
ᴀɪṗ ṗeᴀṫ, during.
Ꭿlbᴀ, Scotland.
Ꭿlbᴀɪnn (*dat.*), Scot-
   land.
ᴀ mᴀṗᴀċ, to-morrow.
ᴀn-ṗóᵹlumċᴀ, very
   learned.
bᴀɪl, prosperity.
beᴀnnuɪᵹɪṫ(may)bless.
b-ṗuɪl, is, are.
cᴀṫ, what.
cᴀoɪ, way.
ceɪṫ (*gen.*), first.
cɪᴀ, who?
cɪᴀnnoṗ, how?
cnoɪc, of a hill.
ċo, so, as.
cómuṗṗᴀ, a neighbour.
ċṗuɪnnɪᵹ (ye), gathered
ṫeᴀcᴀɪṗ, difficult.
ṫeɪṁɪn, certain.
ṫíolᴀnn (*hab.*), sells.
ṗáᵹ (*perf.*) left.
ṗeᴀṫ, a space of time.
ṗéɪṫɪṗ, possible.
ṗlɪuċ, wet.
ṗóᵹlumċᴀ, learned.
ᵹeᴀṗṗ (*v.*), cut.
ᵹeuᵹ, *n. m.*, a branch.

ᵹeuᵹᴀɪb(*dat.*)branches
ᵹlᴀɪṗ (*gen.*), green.
ᵹo ṫeɪṁɪn, indeed.
ᵹo mɪnɪc, oftentimes.
leᴀbᴀɪṗ, (*pl.*) books.
(*gen.*)of a book.
léɪᵹeᴀṫ, reading.
lɪom, with me.
—mᴀṗᴀċ, morrow.
mɪc (*gen and voc.*), son.
míle, a thousand.
mɪnɪc, often.
neᴀṗc, might.
ṗᴀċṗᴀṫ, I will go.
ṗᴀɪb, was (may be).
ṗcṗíob, (who) wrote.
ṗeᴀṗ, *v.* (*past*) stood.
ṗnᴀċᴀṫ, a needle.
ṗoɪṗbɪᵹɪṫ(may)prosper
cᴀɪm, I am.
cᴀɪṗ, thou art.
cᴀmᴀɪll, of a while.
cᴀmᴀll, a while.
cɪᵹ (*dat.*), house.
cú ṗéɪn, thyself.
cuɪᵹṗɪn (*inf.*), (to) understand.
úᵹṫᴀṗ, an author.
Uí Ꭰonnᴀbáɪn, of
   O'Donovan.

1. Ciannoġa b-ᵽuil ċú ?
2. Ciannoᵽ ċáiᵽ,
3. Ciannoᵽ ċá ċú, } How are you ?
4. Caᵯ é maᵽ ċá ċú,
5. Cia ċaoi b-ᵽuil ċú,
6. Ċáim ᴣo maiċ. Ciannoᵽ a b-ᵽuil ċú-ᵽéin ? I am well. How is yourself ?
7. Ċá mé ᴣo maiċ, buiᵭeaċaᵽ leaċ. I am well (thanks with you), thank you.
8. ᴣo ᵽaib maiċ aᴣaċ (may good be to you). Thank you.
9. ᴣo m-beannuiᴣiᵭ Ɗia ᵭuiċ. May God bless you.
10. ᴣo ᵽoiᵽbiᴣiᵭ Ɗia ᵭuiċ. May God prosper you.
11. Bail ó Ɗia oᵽċ, a ṁic mo ċᵽoiᵭe. A blessing from God on you, son of my heart.
12. Ṁo ᵽeaċċ mile beannaċċ oᵽċ. My seven thousand blessings on you.
13. ᴣo m-beannuiᴣiᵭ Ɗia aᵽ n-obaiᵽ. May God bless our work.
14. Iᵽ bᵽeáᴣ an lá é ᵽo. This is a fine day.
15. Béiᵭ ᵽé ᵽliuċ a máᵽaċ. It will be wet to-morrow.
16. Slán leaċ aiᵽ ᵽeaᵭ ċamaill. Farewell for a while.
17. An labᵽann ċú ᴣaeᵭilᴣe ? Do you speak Irish.

18. Tá me ag léigeaḋ an céiꝺ leaḃair. I am reading the First Book.

19. Ní ꝺeacair a ꞇuigrin é. It is not hard to understand it.

20. Ir é rin leaḃar Uí Ḋonnaḃáin. That is O'Donovan's Book.

21. Naċ maiꞇ an ꞇ-úgꝺar a rcríoḃ é? Was it not a good author who wrote it?

22. Buꝺ rear an róglumꞇa é. He was a very learned man.

23. Aꞇḃeoḋuig an ꞇeanga árra. Revive the ancient language.

24. Béiꝺ an gaeḋilge raoi ṁear rór. The Irish will be yet in esteem.

25. Ḃ-ruil ꝺ' aꞇair beo? Is your father alive?

26. Ní ruil; ꞇá ré marḃ. No; he is dead.

27. Tá a ṁáꞇair beo. His mother is alive.

28. Ní ruil a ꝺearḃṫiúr ꞇinn. His sister is not sick.

29. Ḃí mo ꝺearḃráꞇair a Albainn. My brother was in Scotland.

30. Ḃ-ruil ḃur g-cóṁurra ꞇinn? Is your neighbour sick?

31. Do ċruinnig riḃ reur an cnoic glair. Ye gathered the grass of the green hill.

32. An ḃ-ruil ꞇú ag ꝺul gur an m-baile? Are you going to the town?

33. Raċraꝺ air ball iar b-proinn. I will go immediately after dinner.

34. B' ḟéidir go b-fuil sé a d-tiġ an t-sagairt? Perhaps he is in the priest's house?

35. Tá sé faoi ġeugaiḃ na g-crann. He is under the branches of the trees.

36. Raiḃ tú ag an g-carraig? Were you at the rock?

37. D' ḟág mé suas air an t-sliaḃ é. I left him up on the mountain.

38. Gearr geug de'n ċrann. Cut a branch from the tree.

39. Taḃair ḋam an t-snáṫad. Give me the needle.

40. Do ṡeas sé suas air an m-bóṫar. He stood up on the road.

41. Nach í so an ḃean ṁór? Is not this the big woman?

42. Is maiṫ na h-uiḃe a tá aici. She has good eggs (It is good the eggs which are with her).

43. Is maiṫ iad go deiṁin. They are good indeed.

44. Cionnos a ḋíolann tú na leaḃair? How do you sell the books?

45. Ċo saor a's is féidir liom.[1] As cheaply as I can.

46. Is é neart a ḋeunas ceart go minic. It is might which makes right oftentimes.

[1] A's is a contracted form of agus, and is translated "as" in such connexions as the above. It follows ċo, so.

HEADLINES IN COPY-BOOK.

The first thirty-three Headlines consist of the letters and words which occur in the FIRST IRISH BOOK. They present no difficulty to the student; but, as the remaining lines are Irish proverbs, some words which do not occur either in the First or Second Books will be met with in them. These lines are now given here with meaning in English, and the words are incorporated into the vocabulary at end of this book, so that the learner who has studied the First Book and the first portion of the Copy-book may now commence to write out the proverbs, which will be a useful Exercise on the foregoing rules.

An cé le nacᵹ́ruaᵹ ᴅo He who does not pity
  cár, ná ᴅeun ᴅo   your case, do not
  ᵹeapán leiᵣ.   make your com-
                      plaint to him.

bí cneaᵣᴅa ann ᴅo Be honest in all your
  cuiᴅ ᵣáotaiᵣ ᵹo   dealings.
  h-uile.

Cᵣuinniᵹ an ᵱeuᵣ le Make hay while the
  lonnᵣaᴅ na ᵹᵱéine. sun shines.

ᴅeun maᵣ baᴅ mait Do as you would wish
  leat beit ᴅeunta   to be done by.
  leat.

Éiᵣe, na ᴅeoᵣa aᵹuᵣ Erinn, the tears and
  ᵣmíᵹeaᴅa ᴅo ᵱúl.   the smiles of thine
                      eyes.

Feáᵣᵣ coiᵹilt aiᵣ It is better to spare in
  ᴅ-túᵣ ionáaiᵣᴅeiᵣe. the beginning than
                      at the end.

ᵹeall beaᵹán act Promise little, but do
  ᴅeun móᵣán.   much.

ᵹníᴅ taᵣt taᵣt.   Thirst produces thirst.

78

Iꞃ ıonnꬷn ꬷ ꞃeıꞇ mꬷıꞇ It is the same to be
ꬷʒuꞃ ꬷ ꞃeıꞇ ꬷoıꞃ- good as to be happy.
neꬷꞓ.

Leꬷnꬷnn nꬷıꞃe ꬷʒuꞃ Shame and sorrow fol-
ꞃꞃón ꬷn ꞩúꞃꬷılce. low vice.

Mꬷ'ꞃ ꞃꬷꞩꬷ Lꬷ ꞇıʒ If the day be long,
oıꞝꞓe. night comes.

Mꬷıꞃʒ ꞯeꬷLLꬷꞃ ꬷıꞃ ꬷ Woe (to him who) de-
ꞓꬷꞃꬷıꞝ. ceives his friend.

Nı uꬷıꞃLeꬷꞓꞇ ʒꬷn ꞃú- No nobility without
ꞃꬷılce. virtue.

Nı ꞃ-ꞯuıL ꞃꬷoı ʒꬷn There is no sage with-
Loꞓꞇ. out a fault.

OLc ꞃíon nꬷꞓ mꬷıꞇ A bad blast, which is
ꞝ' ꬷón. not good for (some)
one.

Oꞇꞃꬷꞃ ꞃóʒ ꬷn Leꬷʒꬷ. Illness (is) the comfort of the physician.

Pꞃíoṁ ꞃıꬷʒꬷıL ꞃeꬷꞓꬷ The fear of God (is)
eꬷʒLꬷ ꞝé. the first rule of life.

Rún ʒꬷꞓ ꞃeꬷꞃc ꬷn ꞃıʒ The desire of every
ceꬷꞃꞇ. love (is) the rightful
king.

Rꬷnn, ꞃꬷnnꬷıꞝ. A song, a songster.

Seꬷꞓꬷın Luꞓꞇ ꞝeunꞇꬷ Shun those who make
ꬷn ꬷꞓꞃꬷınn. contention.

Coꞃꬷꞓ ꞯLꬷꞓꬷ ꞯꬷılꞇe. The beginning of a
prince (is) greeting.

Coꞃꬷꞓ ꞃLꬷınꞇe coꞝ- The beginning of
Lꬷꞝ. health (is) sleep.

Ꝺaṁan Ꝺé cor eaꜱna The fear of God (is) the
é.   beginning of wis-
                        dom.

Uṁláċc ꝺ' uairleáċc. Humility to nobleness.

NOTE.

The inflections or changes of termination
which nouns and verbs undergo in Irish will
appear strange to the learner who has no knowledge of any language but English. We have
not in this book entered into any explanation
of the rules by which they are governed, but
have, even at some waste of space, given in
the Vocabulary at the end all the inflected
forms which were necessary for our present
purpose. When the learner comes to understand the Rules of Declension and Conjugation he will not require this aid.

The following explanation will for the present be sufficient :—

The Nominative case is the same as the
Nominative in English.

The Genitive is like the Possessive.

The Dative is like the Objective, governed
by a preposition, which is *always* used with
this case in Irish.

The Accusative case is the same as the Objective.

The Vocative case corresponds to the Nominative *of address* in English.

ABBREVIATIONS
USED IN VOCABULARY.

acc. accusative.
adj. adjective.
adv. adverb.
cond. conditiona!.
conj. conjunction.
dat. dative.
dem. demonstrative.
emph. emphatic.
f. feminine.
fut. future.
gen. genitive.
hab. habitual.
imp. imperative.
indic. indicative.
inf. infinitive.
int. interrogative.
intens. intensitive.
interj. interjection.
m. masculine.
n. noun.
neg. negative.

nom. nominative.
num. numeral.
opt. optative.
ord. ordinal.
par. particle.
part. participle.
pass. passive.
pers. person.
pl. plural.
poss. possessive.
prep. preposition.
pron. pronoun.
pr. pron. prepositional
  pronoun.
pres. present.
reit. reiterative.
rel. relative.
sing. singular.
subj. subjunctive.
voc. vocative

VOCABULARY OF ALL WORDS IN THIS BOOK.

ᴀ, *poss. pron.* his, her, its, their.

ᴀ, *rel. pron.* who, which.

ᴀ (sign of infin.), to.

ᴀ, *intrj.*)sign of voc.), o.

ᴀ, *prep.* in.

ᴀbᴘán, *n m.* a song.

ᴀbᴘᴀin, *n. m. pl.* songs.

ᴀcᴀ, *pr. pron.* at or with them.

ᴀċᴘᴀinn, *n. m. gen.* of contention.

ᴀċᴘᴀnn, *n. m.* contention.

ᴀċᴄ, *conj.* but.

ᴀᴅ, *n. m.* luck.

ᴀᴅᴀᴘc, *n. f.* a horn.

ᴀᴅᴀᴘcᴀ, *n. f. pl.* horns.

ᴀᴅᴍᴜᴅ, *n. m.* timber.

ᴀ͛, *prep.* at, with.

ᴀ͛, sign of participle.

ᴀ͛ᴀib, *pr. pron.* at you.

ᴀ͛ᴀiᴅ, *n. f.* a face.

ᴀ͛ᴀinn, *pr. pron.* at us.

ᴀ͛ᴀm, *pr. pron.* at me.

ᴀ͛ᴀᴄ, *pr. pron.* at thee.

ᴀ͛ᴜᴘ, *conj* and.

ᴀici, *pr. pron.* at (or with) her

ᴀil, *n. f.* will, pleasure.

ᴀill, *n. f.* a cliff.

ᴀille, *n. f. gen.* of a cliff

ᴀilleᴀċc, *n. f.* beauty.

ᴀimᴘiᴘ, *n. f.* time, season

ᴀinm, *n. m.* a name.

ᴀiᴘ, *prep.* on, upon.

ᴀiᴘ, *pr. pron.* on him.

ᴀiᴘ bᴀll, *adv. phrase,* on the spot, by-and-by

ᴀiᴘ ᴘeᴀᴅ, *adv.* during.

ᴀiᴘ͛ioᴅ, *n. m.* silver, money.

ᴀiᴘiᴅ͛ce, *adj.* special.

ᴀiᴘmᴀioin, *adv. phrase* in the morning.

ᴀiᴘ ᴅ-ᴄúᴘ, *adv. phrase,* in the beginning.

ᴀic, *n. f.* a place.

ᴀl, *n. m.* a brood.

ᴀlbᴀ, *n. f.* Scotland.

ᴀlbᴀinn, *dat.* (in) Scotland.

ᴀluinn, *adj.* beautiful.

ᴀm, *n. m.* time.

ᴀmᴀċ, *adv.* out.

ᴀmᴀil *suffix.* (*al.*), like

ᴀmáin, *adv.* only, alone

ᴀ máᴘᴀċ, *adv* tomorrow

Ⰰ m-baile, *adv.* at home (see 'r ⱍn m-baile).

Ⰰmuⰺⰷ, *adv.* outside.

Ⰰn, *article*, the.

Ⰰn, *int. par.* whether?

Ⰰn, *neg. par.* (*in* or *un*) not.

Ⰰn, *intens. par.* very.

Ⰰnⰰm, *n. m.* a soul.

Ⰰnⰰṁ, *adv.* seldom.

Ⰰn-ḃreⰰⰷ, *adj.* very fine

Ⰰnrⰰ, *n. m.* a storm.

Ⰰn-ḟóⰷlumⱍⰰ, *part. adj.* very learned.

Ⰰníor, *adv.* up (from below).

Ⰰn-ṁaⰉⱅ, *adj.* very good

Ⰰnn, *prep.* in.

Ⰰnn, *pr. pron.* in him, in it.

Ⰰnn, *adv.* there, therein

Ⰰnnr, *prep.* in.

Ⰰnn rⰉn, *adv.* there (in that), then.

Ⰰnn ro, *adv.* here, in this

Ⰰnn rúⰑ, *adv.* there, yonder.

ⰀnoⰉr, *adv.* now.

Ⰰnróⰷ, *n. m.* misery.

Ⰰnuⰰr, *adv.* down (from above).

ⰀoⰉḃneⰰċ, *adj.* glad, happy.

ⰀoⰉr, *n. f.* age.

Ⰰon, *num.* one.

Ⰰon-Ⱁeuⰷ, *num.* eleven.

Ⰰonṁⰰ⸱Ⱃ, *ord. num.* first

ⰀonmⰰⰑ-Ⱁeuⰷ, *ord. num.* eleventh.

Ⰰoroⰰ, *adj.* old, aged.

Ⰰr, *poss. pron.* our.

Ⰰr, *int. par.* whether?

Ⰰr, *rel. pron.* who, what (before past tense).

Ⰰrán, *n. m.* bread.

ⰀrⰑ, *adj.* high, loud.

ⰀrⰑeⰰrroⰷ, *n. m.* an Archbishop.

ⰀrⰑ-ṁeⰰr, *n. m.* high regard.

ⰀroⱃⰉⰷ, *n. m.* a high king, a monarch.

Ⰰrrⰰ, *adj.* ancient.

ⰀroⱃcoⰉl, *n. f.* a high school, a college.

Ⰰr, *prep.* out of.

Ⰰ'r (*cont.* for ⰰⰷur), as, and.

Ⰰrⱅeⰰċ, *adv.* in, into.

ⰀrⱅⰉⰷ, *adv.* inside.

Ⰰⱅ, *reit. par.* (*re*) again

ⰀⱅⰰⰉr, *n. m.* a father.

Aċap, *n. m. gen.* of a father.

Aċbeoúuiġ, *verb*, revive

ba, *n. f. pl.* cows.

ba, *v.* (past indic. of ip) was ; see buó.

báó, *n. m.* a boat.

baó (*condit. of* ip) may be, was.

bail, *n. f.* prosperity, success.

baile, *n. m.* (*nom.* and *gen.*) a town.

báin, *adj. gen.* of bán, white.

bainṗeip, *n. f.* a wedding.

bainpíoġan, *n. f.* a queen.

bainċiġeapna, *n. f.* a lady, a chieftainess.

báipo, *n. m. gen.* of a bard.

baipeuo, *n. m.* a hat.

bán, *adj.* white.

baoġal, *n. m.* danger.

baoip, *n. f.* folly.

bápo, *n. m.* a bard.

bápp, *n. m.* the top.

beaċ, *n. f.* a bee.

beaġ, *adj.* little.

beaġán, *n. m.* a little, a few.

bean, *n. f.* a woman.

beannaċt, *n. f.* a blessing.

beannuiġ, *v. imp.* bless

beannuiġió, *v.* (*opt.*) (may) bless.

béappaó, *v.* (*cond.*), would give.

beaċa, *n. f.* (*nom.* and *gen.*) life.

beió, *v.* (*fut.*) will be.

beip, *v.* (*imp.*) bring.

beiċ, *v.* (*inf.*) to be.

beiċ, *n. f.* a being.

beo, *adj.* living, alive.

beoúuiġ, *v.* (*imp.*) animate.

beupaċ, *adj.* mannered

b-ṗuil, *v.* (*int.*) is, are ?

bi, *v.* (*imp.*) be.

bi, *adj.*, *gen.* of beo, living.

bi, *v.* (*past indic.*) was.

bióeap, *v.* (1st *pers. sing. past*), I was.

biġ, *adj.* (*gen.* and *voc.* of beaġ), little.

binn, *adj.* melodious, harmonious.

bíooaṗ (*3rd pers. pl. past*), they were.

blaṙ, *n. m.* taste.

bláṫ, *n. m.* a blossom.

bliaoáin, *n.f.* a year.

bó, *n.f.* a cow.

boċt, *adj.* poor.

bóṫaṗ, *n. m.* a road.

bóṫaṗ-iaṗain, *n. m.* a railroad.

bṗáṫ, *n. m.* judgment; see ʒo bṗáṫ.

bṗáṫaiṗ,*n.m.*a brother

bṗeac, *adj.* speckled.

bṗeáʒ, *adj.* fine, fair.

bṗian, *n. m.* Brian.

bṗiain, *n. m. gen.* of Brian.

bṗic, *adj.gen.* of bṗeac speckled.

bṗíʒ, *n. f.* essence.

bṗíʒoe, *n. f. gen.* of Brigid.

bṗíʒio, *n. f.* Brigid.

bṗirte,*partadj.*broken

bṗóʒ, *n. f.* a shoe.

bṗóʒa, *n. f. pl.* shoes.

bṗón, *n. m.* sorrow.

buacaill, *n. m.* a cowboy, a boy.

buacalla, *n. m. gen.* of a boy, cowboy.

buaoaiṗt, *n.f.* trouble

buail, *v.* (*imp.*) strike.

buail, *v.* (*past indic.*) (he) struck.

buaileann, *v.* (*hab.*) does strike.

buaileaṙ,*v.* (*rel.pres.*) (who) strikes.

buaileaṙ,*1st per. sing past,* I struck.

buailṗinn, *v.* (*cond.*) I would strike.

buailió, *v.* (*opt.*) may strike.

bualaó, *v.* (*inf.*) to strike.

buan, *adj.* lasting.

buanṡaoʒalaċ, *adj.* long lived.

buanṡearṁaċ, *adj* persevering.

buó, was ; see ba.

buíoe, *adj.* yellow.

buíoeaċ, *adj.* thankful

buíoeaċaṙ,*n.m.*thanks gratitude.

buṗ, *post.pron.* your.

Cá, *int. par.* where ?

Ca, *neg. par.* not.

Cao, *int. adv.* what.

Ċaill, *v.* (*past indic.*) lost.

Ċailleaṛ, *v.* (*rel. pres.*) (who) loses.

Cait, *n. m. gen.* of a cat

Caiṫ, *v.* spend, eat, use

Caitilín, *n.f.* Catherine

Caoċ, *adj.* blind.

Caoi, *n. m.* way.

Caoin, *adj.* gentle, mild

Caoirḟeoil, *n.f.* mutton

Caoṁ, *adj.* kind, gentle

Caoṁa, *adj., pl.* of caoṁ, kind, soft.

Caora, *n. f.* a sheep.

Capaill, *n. m. gen.* of a horse.

Capall, *n.m.* a horse.

Cara,) *n. m.* and *f.*

Carad,) a friend.

Caraid, *n. m. dat.* of cara.

Carraiġ, *n.f.* a rock.

Cás, *n. m.* a case.

Cat, *n. m.* a cat.

Caṫ, *n. m.* a battle.

Caṫa, *n. m. gen.* of a battle.

Caṫair, *n. f.* a city.

Caṫḃárr, *n.m.* a helmet

Céad, *num.* a hundred.

Ceudna, *adj.* same.

Ceann, *n. m.* a head.

Ceanntíre, *n.m.* a headland.

Ceannuíde, *n. m.* a merchant.

Ceannuiġ, *v.* (*imp.*) buy.

Ċeannuiġ, *v. past indic.* bought.

Cearc, *n. f.* a hen.

Ceart, *n. m.* right.

Ceaṫair, *num.* four.

Ceaṫair-déuġ, *num.* fourteen.

Ceaṫramhaḋ, *ord. num* fourth.

Ceaṫramhaḋ-déuġ, *ord. num.* fourteenth.

Céid, *num.* (*gen.* of ceud), first.

Céin, *adj.* (*dat.* of cian), distant.

Céird, *n. f.* a trade.

Céirde, *n. f. gen.* of a trade.

Céiṫre, *num.* four (with noun).

Ceiṫre-déuġ, *num.* fourteen (with noun).

Ceoil, *n.m. gen.* of music

Ceol, *n. m.* music.

Ceuṫ, *ord. num.* first.

Ceuṫ-ṗṗoinn, *n. f.* breakfast, first meal.

Cia, *int. pron.* who?

Cian, *adj.* far distant.

Cianoṗ, *adj.* how?

Cill, *n. f.* a church.

Ciṗoe, (*nom.* and *gen.*) a chest.

Claṫaiṗe, *n. m.* a coward.

Cláiṫeaṁ, *n. m.* a sword.

Cláiṗ, *n. m. gen.* of a table.

Cláṗ, *n. m.* a table, a board.

Cleaṗ, *n.m.* craft, a trick

Cléiṫ, *n. m. gen.* of a bosom.

Cliaḃ, *n. m.* the chest, bosom.

Cliṗce, *adj.* expert, active.

Cloc, *n. f.* a stone.

Clocaiṗe, *n. m.* a stone-cutter.

Cloṫ, *n.m.* a print, type

Cloṫḃuail, *v.* (*imp.*) print.

Cloṫḃuailce, *part. adj.* printed.

Cloẓ, *n. m.* a bell.

Cloẓceaċ, *n. m.* a bell-house.

Cluaṗ, *n. f.* an ear.

Cneaṗoa, *adj.* honest.

Cnoic, *n.m.gen.* of a hill

Co, *adv.* so, as.

Cooláṫ, *n. m.* sleep.

Coẓáṫ, *n. m.* war.

Coẓaiṫ, *n.m.gen.* of war

Coẓaṗ, *n. m.* a whisper

Coiẓilc *v.* (*inf.*) (to) spare.

Cóiṗ, *adj.* just, right.

Coiṗe, *n.m.* a cauldron

Colann, *n. f.* the body.

Coṁuṗṗa, *n.f.* a neighbour.

Coṗcaċ, *n. f.* Cork

Coṗcaiẓe, *n. f. gen.* of Cork

Copp, *n. m.* a body

Coṗ, *n. f.* a foot

Coṗẓ, *v.* (*inf*) to check

Cṗainn, *n. m. gen.* of a tree.

Cṗann, *n. m.* a tree.

Cṗuaṫaiṗe, *n. m.* a labourer.

Cɲíc, *n. f.* a country.
Cɲíoc, *n. f.* end.
Cɲóḃa, *adj.* valiant.
Cɲoíḋe, *n. m.* a heart.
Cɲuınnıġ, *v. imp.* gather
Cɲuınnıġ, *v.* (*past.indic*) gathered.
Cú, *n.m.* and *f.* a hound
Cuġam, *pr. pron.* to me unto me.
Cuıḋ, *n. f.* a portion, a share.
Cúıġ, *num,* five.
Cúıġ-ḋeuġ, *num.* fifteen
Cúıġeaḋ, *ord.num.* fifth
Cúıġeaḋ - ḋeuġ, *ord. num.* fifteenth.
Cuıɲ, *v.* (*imp.*) put.
Cuıɲle, *n. f.* a vein, a pulse.
Ċum, *com. prep.* (ḋo understood) towards, unto.
Cúṁanġ, *adj.* narrow.
Cú-maɲa, *n. m.* a sea-dog.
Cuɲ, *v.* (*inf.*) to put.
Ḋá, *conj.* if.
Ḋ'a, for ḋo a, to his, to her.
Ḋá, *num.* two.
Ḋá-ḋeuġ, *num.* twelve
Ḋáıl, *n. f.* a meeting.
Ḋaıɲ, *n. f.* an oak.
Ḋam, *pr.pron.* to me
Ḋaṁ, *n. m.* an ox.
Ḋán, *n. m.* a poem.
Ḋaoıne, *n.m.pl.* people
Ḋaɲa, *ord.num.* second
Ḋaɲa-ḋeuġ, *ord. num.* twelfth.
Ḋé, *n.m. gen.* of God.
Ḋe, *prep.* of, off, from.
Ḋeaċaıḋ, *v.* (*subj.*) went
Ḋeacaıɲ, *adj.* difficult.
Ḋeaċṁaḋ, *ord. num.* tenth.
Ḋeaġ, *adj.* good.
Ḋeaġḋuıne, *n.m.* a good man, a good person.
Ḋeaġ-ɲíġ, *n. m.* a good king.
Ḋeaɲḃ, *ad.* real, genuine
Ḋeaɲḃɲáċaıɲ, *n. m.* a brother, a real brother
Ḋeaɲġ, *adj.* red.
Ḋeaɲḃɲúɲ, *n.f.* a sister
Ḋe ḃɲıġ, *conj.* because
Ḋeıċ, *num.* ten.
Ḋeıṁın, *adj.* certain.
Ḋeıɲe, } *n.m.* an end
Ḋeıɲeaḋ, }

Ɗeıꞃ5, *adj. gen.* of Ɗoċaꞃ, *n.m.* loss, harm
  ꝺeaꞃ5, red. Ɗóċaꞃ, *n. m.* hope.
Ɗeoꞃ, *n. m.* a tear. Ɗó-ꝺeu5, *num.* twelve.
Ɗeoꞃa, *n. m. plu.* tears Ɗóꝺeunꞇa, *part. adj.*
Ɗeu5, *num.* teen.   impossible.
Ɗeun, *v.(imp.)* make, do Ɗóᵹeıcꞃıonaċ, *adj.* in-
Ɗeunaꝺ, *v. (inf.)* to do   visible.
Ɗeunaꞃ, *v. (rel. pres.)* Ɗóıb, *pr. pron.* to them
  (who) does. Ɗóṁnaıll, *n.m. gen.* of
Ɗeunꞇa, *n. m. gen.* of   Donal.
  making. Ɗóṁnall, *n. m.* Donal,
Ɗeunꞇa, *pass.par.* done   Daniel.
Ɗıa, *n. m.* God. Ɗona, *adj.* wretched,
Ɗıbꞃeaꝺ, *n. m.* exile.   unfortunate.
Ɗılıꞃ, *adj.* dear, fond. Ɗonn, *adj.* brown.
Ɗıolann, *v. (hab.)* sells. Ɗoꞃaꞃ, *n. m.* a door.
Ɗıom, *pr. pron.* off or Ɗoꞃn, *n. m.* a fist.
  from me. Ɗꞃıꞃeo5, *n.f.* a brier.
Ɗıoꞇ, *pr. pron.* off or Ɗub, *adj.* black.
  from thee. Ɗúbaılce, *n. f.* vice.
Ɗc, *prep.* to. Ɗuılle, *n. m.* a leaf.
Ɗo, *poss. pron.* thy. Ɗuıne, *n. m.* a man, a
Ɗo, *num.* two.   person.
Ɗó *prefix,* implying Ɗuınn, *pr. pron.* to us.
  difficulty. Ɗuıꞇ, *pr. pron.* to thee
Ɗó, *pr. pron.* to him. Ɗul, *v. ⁽inf.⁾* to go
Ɗo, *par.* used before   going.
  certain tenses. Ɗún, *v. (imp.)* shut.
Ɗo, *sign of inf.* to. Ɗún, *v.(past indic.)* shut
Ɗóbeuꞃaċ, *adj.* ill- Ɗúnaꝺ, *v. (inf.)* to shut
  mannered Ɗúnꞇa, *pass. part.* shut

é, *pers. pron.* he, him, it

eᴀċ, *n. m.* a steed.

eᴀʒlᴀ, *n. f.* fear.

eᴀʒnᴀ, *n. f.* wisdom.

eıċ, *n. m. pl.* steeds.

éıpe, *n. f.* Ireland.

éıpeᴀnn, *n. f. gen.* of Ireland.

éıpınn, *n. f. dat.* (in) Ireland.

eıcıllım, *v.* (1st *sing. pres.*) I fly.

eıcleᴀ́ʋ, *n. m.* flight.

eolᴀp, *n.m.* knowledge, skill.

euʋᴀċ, *n. m.* clothes.

eun, *n. m.* a bird, a fowl.

fᴀ, *prep.* under ; see fᴀoı.

fᴀʋ, *adj.* distant ; ᴀ ḃfᴀʋ, *adv.* far away.

fᴀʋᴀ, *adj.* long.

fᴀ́ʒ, *v.* (*imp.*) leave.

fᴀ́ʒ, *v.* (*past indic.*) left.

fᴀ́ılce, *n. f.* greeting.

fᴀ́ınne, *n. m.* a ring.

fᴀıpʒe, *n. f.* the sea.

faıppınʒ, *adj.* wide.

fᴀn, *v.* (*imp.*) stay.

fᴀoı, *prep.* under.

fᴀol, *adj.* wild.

fᴀol-ċú, *n. m.* a wolf.

fᴀ ċuᴀıpım, *adv. phrase* towards.

feᴀʋ, *n. f.* a space of time.

ḟeᴀllᴀp, *v.* (*rel. pres.*) (who) deceives.

feᴀp, *n. m.* a man.

feᴀpᴀıḃ, *n. m. dat. pl.* (to) men.

feᴀpᴀṁᴀıl, *adj.* manly

feᴀpᴀnn, *n. m.* a field, land.

feᴀp-ceoıl, *n. m.* a musician.

feᴀp-feᴀpᴀ, *n. m.* a seer, a wizard.

feᴀpp, *comp. adj.* better

feᴀpᴀ, *n. m. gen.* of knowledge.

feıceᴀnn, *v.* (*hab.*) sees, does see.

féıʋıp, *adj.* possible.

féın, *emph. pron.* self, own.

feoıl, *n. f.* flesh, meat

feup, *n. m.* grass, hay.

fıᴀċ, *n. m.* a raven.

fıᴀʋ, *n. m.* a deer.

fıċe, *num.* twenty.

fıċeᴀ́ʋ, *num.* twentieth

Fíle, *n. m.* a poet.

Fíleaḋ, *n. m. gen. pl.* of poets.

Fíon, *n. m.* wine.

Fíona, *n. m. gen.* of wine.

Fíor, *adj.* true.

Fíorḃuan, *adj.* steadfast.

Fíor-ċara, *n. m.* or *f.* a true friend.

Fíoróiliṡ, *adj.* sincere.

Fíos, *n. m.* knowledge.

Fir, *n. m. (gen. and voc)* of a man.

Fir, *n. m. pl.* men.

Flaiṫ, *n. m.* a prince.

Flaṫa, *n. m. gen.* of a prince.

Fliuċ, *adj.* wet.

Focail, *n. m. (gen.* and *pl.)* words.

Focal, *n. m.* a word.

Fóġluim, *v.(imp.)* learn.

Fóġluim, *v. (inf.)* to learn.

Fóġlumṫa, *adj.* learned

Fóġaiṙ, *v. (imp.)* warn.

Fóġraḋ, *v.(inf.)* to warn

Foġus, *adj.* near ; a b-foġus, *adv.* near.

Foiġíd, } *n. f.* patience.
Foiġíde, }

Foillríġ, *v. (imp.)* show, publish.

Foillríġeann, *v. (hab.)* shows.

Foillríġeaṙ, *v. (past indic.)* I showed.

Follaṁ, *adj.* empty.

Fór, *adv.* yet.

Forgailte, *pass. part.* opened.

Fuaim, *n. f.* a sound.

Fuair, *adj.gen.of* fuar, cold.

Fuar, *adj.* cold.

Fuil, *n. f.* blood.

Fuil, *v. (subj.)* am.

Fuilim, *v. (subj.)* I am.

Fuinneog, *n.f.* a window

Fulaing, *v.(imp.)* suffer

Fulang, *v.(inf.)* to suffer

Gaḃ, *v. (imp.)* take, seize.

Gabáil, *v. (inf.)* to take, taking.

Gabaṙ, *n. m.* a goat.

Gaċ, *adj. pron.* each, every.

Gaḋuiḋe, *n. m. (nom. and gen.)* a thief.

Ᵹᴀᴇᴏ́ɪʟɪᴣ, Ᵹᴀᴇᴏ́ɪʟᴣᴇ, *n. f.* Gaelic (the language of the Irish and of the Highland Scotch.)

Ᵹᴀɪʟ, *n. f.* steam, vapour.

Ᵹᴀɪʟᴇ, *n.f.gen.* of steam

Ᵹᴀɴ, *prep.* without.

Ᵹᴀᴏᴄ̇, *n. f.* wind.

Ᵹᴀṗḃ, *adj.* rough, rugged.

Ᵹᴇᴀʟ, *adj.* bright, white

Ᵹᴇᴀʟʟ, *n. m.* a pledge, a promise.

Ᵹᴇᴀʟʟ, *v.(imp.)* promise.

Ᵹᴇᴀṗṗ, *v. (imp.)* cut.

Ᵹᴇᴀṗᴀ́ɴ, *n. m.* a complaint.

Ᵹᴇᴀṗṗṗɪᴀᴏ̇, *n. m.* a hare.

Ᵹᴇɪɴᴇᴀʟᴀᴄ̇, *n. m.* a generation.

Ᵹᴇɪɴᴇᴀʟᴀɪᴣᴇ, *n. m. pl.* generations.

Ᵹᴇᴜᴣ, *n. f.* a branch.

Ᵹᴇᴜᴣᴀɪḃ, *n. f. (dat.)* branches.

Ᵹᴇᴜṗ, *adj.* sharp.

Ᵹɪʟ, *adj.(voc. of* ᴣᴇᴀʟ*)*, bright.

Ᵹɪᴏʟʟᴀ, *n.m.* a servant.

Ᵹʟᴀᴄ, *v. (imp.)* take, receive.

Ᵹʟᴀɪṗ, *adj. (gen.)* green

Ᵹʟᴀṗ, *adj.* green.

Ᵹʟᴀṗ, *n. m.* a lock.

Ᵹʟᴇᴏᴏ̇ᴀᴄ̇, *adj.* noisy, quarrelsome.

Ᵹʟɪᴄ, *adj.* cunning, wise

Ᵹɴɪᴏ̇, *v.* makes.

Ᵹɴᴏ́, *n. m. (nom. and gen.)* work, business.

Ᵹᴏ, *prep.* unto, till.

Ᵹᴏ, *par. before verbs,* that.

Ᵹᴏ, *par.,* before an adjective forms an adverb.

Ᵹᴏ ḃṗᴀᴄ̇, *adv.* for ever.

Ᵹᴏ ᴏᴇɪṁɪɴ, *adv.* indeed

Ᵹᴏ mᴀɪᴄ̇, *adv.* well.

Ᵹᴏ mɪɴɪᴄ, *adv.* oftentimes.

Ᵹᴏṗᴄ, *n. m.* a field, a garden.

Ᵹᴏ ᴛṗᴏm, *adv.* heavily

Ᵹᴏ h-ᴜɪʟᴇ, *adv.* wholly.

Ᵹṗᴀᴏ̇, *n. m.* love.

Ᵹṗᴀᴏ̇ᴜɪᴣ, *v.(imp.)* love.

Spéine, *n. f. gen.* of the sun.

Sṁan, *n. f.* the sun.

Suiḋ, *v. (imp.)* pray.

Suiḋe, *v. (inf.)* to pray.

Suiḋe, *n. f.* prayer.

Sup, *par. before verbs*, that.

Sup, *prep.* unto, towards

i, *prep.* in; see ɑ.

í, *pers. pron.* she, her.

iɑᴅ, *pers. pron.* they, them.

iɑp, *prep.* after.

iɑpɑin, *n.m.gen.* of iron.

iɑpɑn, *n. m.* iron.

iɑpɡ, *n. m.* a fish.

iḃ, *pers. pron.* you, ye.

ioip, *prep.* between.

Inɡeɑn, *n. f.* a daughter

Inɡeɑnɑ, *n.f.pl.* daughters.

inn, *pers. pron.* we, us.

inneopɑᴅ, *v. (1st. sing. fut.)* I will tell.

innip, *v. (imp.)* tell.

inpe, *n. f. gen.* of an island.

ion, *prefix,* expressing fitness.

ioná, *adv.* than.

ionᴅeunтɑ, *part. adj.* fit to be done, practicable.

ionṁuin, *adj.* dear, beloved.

ionnɑn, *adj.* equal.

ir, *prep.* in; see i.

ir, *v. (assertive)* is.

Lá, *n. m.* a day.

Lɑḃpɑnn, *v.(hab.)* does speak.

Láiᴅip, *adj.* strong.

Láṁ, *n. f.* a hand.

Lán, *adj.* full.

Lán, *n. m.* the full.

Lɑoċ, *n. m.* a hero.

Lɑoɡ, *n. m.* a calf.

Lɑoɡ-mɑpɑ, *n.m.* a sea calf.

Lɑoiɡpeoil, *n. f.* veal.

Le, *prep,* with.

Leɑḃɑip, *n. m. gen.* of a book.

Leɑḃɑip, *n.m.pl.* books

Leɑḃɑp, a book.

Leɑɡɑ, *n. m. gen.* of a physician.

Leɑn, *v. (imp.)* follow.

Leɑnɑnn, *v. (hab.)* follows.

Leɑnḃ. *n. m.* a child.

Leac, *pr. pron.* with thee.

Leaċ, *n.f.* half.

Leaċṁaṙb, *adj.* half dead.

Léiᵹeaḋ, *pres. part.* reading.

Léim, *n.f.* a leap.

Leinb, *n. m. pl.* children.

Leiṙ, *prep.* with ; see Le

Leiṙ, *pr. pron.* with him

Liaiᵹ, *n.m.* a physician

Liaċ, *adj.* gray.

Lib, *pr. pron.* with you.

Liom, *pr. pron.* with me

Lion, *v. (imp.)* fill.

Lion, *v. (past indic.)* filled.

Lobċa, *pass.part.* rotten

Loċ, *n. m.* a lake, lough.

Loċc, *n. f.* a fault.

Loᵹ, *n. m.* a hollow.

Lonᵹ, *n.f.* a ship.

Lonᵹ-coᵹaiḋ, *n. f.* a ship of war.

Lonᵹ-ᵹaile, *n. f.* a steamboat.

Lonᵹṗoṗ, ᴞ *m.* a camp, a fort.

Lonnṗaḋ, *n.m* shining.

Luaċ, *n. m.* a price.

Luaċṁaṙ, *adj.* precious

Lúb, *v. (imp.)* bend.

Lúbċa, *pass.part.* bent, looped.

Luċ, *n.f.* a mouse.

Luċc, *n.m.* folk.

Luib, *n. f.* an herb, a plant.

Luibᵹoṙc, *n. m.* a garden, herb garden.

Má, *conj.* if.

Mac, *n. m.* a son.

Mac-alla, *n.m.* an echo

Maḋaḋ, ⎫
Maoṗaḋ, ⎭ *n.m.* a dog.

Maᵹaḋ, *n. m.* mocking

Maṙoin, *n, f.* the morning.

Maiᵹᴅean, *n. f.* a maiden.

Maiṙ, *v. (imp.)* live.

Máiṙe, *n.f.* Mary.

Maiṙᵹ, *n.f.* woe.

Maiṙcṙeoil, *n.f.* beef.

Maiċ, *v. imp.* forgive.

Ṁaiċ, *v. past indic.* forgave.

Maiċ, *adj.* good.

Mála, *n. m. (nom. and gen.)* a bag.

6

Manać, *n. m.* a monk.
Manaıġ, *n. m.* gen. of a monk.
Maol, *adj.* bald.
Maol, *n. m.* a votary.
Map, *prep.* like to, as.
Map, *adv.* as.
Map, *suffix.* (*al.*) like.
Mapa, *n. f. gen.* of the sea.
Mápać, *n. m.* morrow.
Mapb, *adj.* dead.
Mapb, *v.* (*imp.*)kill,slay
Map ṙın, *adv.*so, as that
Mapc, *n. m.* a beef.
Mapċaın, *v.* (*inf.*) to live.
Má'ṙ (i.e. má ıṙ) it is.
Máċaıp, *n. f.* a mother
Mé, *pers. pron.* I, me.
Meall, *v.* (*imp.*) deceive.
Meallaṙ, *v.* (*rel. pres.*) deceives.
Meaṙ, *n. m.* esteem.
Méıd, *n. f.* size.
Mı, } *n. f.* a month.
Mıoṙ, }
Mıc, (*gen. and voc.*)son
Mıċeál, *n.m.* Michael.
Mıċıl, *gen.* of Michael

Mıl, *n. f.* honey.
Mıle, *num.* a thousand
Mılıṙ, *adj.* sweet.
Mın, *n. f.* meal.
Mın, *adj.* fine, smooth.
Mınıc, *adj.* often.
Mıoṙa, *n. f. pl.* months
Mıṙe, *pers. pron.emph.* I, myself.
Mná, *n. f. pl.* women.
Mnáıb, *n. f. dat. pl.* women.
Mnaoı, *n. f. dat.* (to) a woman.
Mo, *poss. pron.* my.
Móıṙ, *adj.* (*gen.of* móṙ) great.
Móṙ, *adj.* great, large.
Móṙa, *adj. pl.* big.
Móṙán, *n. m.* much, many.
Móṙpıan, *n.f.*greatpain
Móṙṙeol, *n. m.* a great sail, a mainsail.
Móṙ-ċaṙc, *n. m.* great thirst.
Muc, *n. f.* a pig.
Mucṙeoıl, *n. f.* pork, bacon, swine-flesh.
Munncıṙ, *n. f.* people.
Muıṙ, *n. f.* the sea.

ꞹullꞁꞇ,*n.m.*top,sum-
mit.

ꞹunꞁ, *conj.* unless.

ꞹunꞁ, *conj.* (with past
tense) unless.

ꞹúꞃꞡꞁꞁl,*v.(imp)*waken

Ꞁꞁ, *article (pl.* or *gen.*
fem.) the.

Ꞁꞁꞇ, *int. par.* whether
not.

Ꞁꞁꞇ, *neg, par.* that not,
who not.

Ꞁꞁꞇꞁꞃ, *par.* (with past
tense) that not.

Ꞁáꞁꞁe, *n. f.* shame.

Ꞁꞁoꞁ, *num.* nine.

Ꞁꞁoꞁꝺeuꞡ, *num.* nine-
teen.

Ꞁꞁoꞁ, *n.m.* a saint.

Ꞁꞁoꞁꞁꝺ*ord.num.*ninth

Ꞁꞁoꞁꞁꝺ - ꝺeuꞡ, *ord.*
num. nineteenth.

Ꞁꞁoꞁꞇꞁ, *adj.* holy.

Ꞁá'ꞁ, *par.* that not.

Ꞁeꞁꞁ,*neg.par.*(un*or*in)

Ꞁeꞁꞁꞇꞁꞁbeꞁꞇ, *adj.*
unprofitable.

Ꞁeꞁꞁꞇꞁꞃócꞁꞁeꞁꞇ, *adj.*
unmerciful.

Ꞁeꞁꞃꞇ, *n. m.* might.

Ꞁꞁ. *neg. adv.* not.

Ꞁꞁ (*cont. for* ꞁꞡeꞁn), a
daughter.

Ꞁꞁoꞁ, *neg. par.* (with
past tense) not.

Ꞁo, *conj.* or, nor.

Ꞁóꞃ, *n. m.* habit, cus-
tom, fashion.

Ꞁ, *prep.* from.

O (*form of* uꞁ)a grand-
son, descendant, pre-
fixed to family names.

Obꞁꞁꞁ, *n. f.* work.

Obꞁꞁꞁ-ꞇeꞁne,*n.f.*a fire-
work.

Obꞁꞁꞁ-uꞁꞁꞡe *n. f.* a
waterwork.

Ocꞁꞁꞃ, *n. m.* hunger.

Oꞇꞇ, *num.* eight.

Oꞇꞇꝺeuꞡ*num.*eighteen

Oꞇꞇmꞁꝺ, *ord. num.*
eighth.

Oꞇꞇmꞁꝺ - ꝺeuꞡ, *ord.*
num. eighteenth.

Óꞡ, *adj.* young.

Oꞁóꞇe, *n. f.* night.

Óꞁꞡ, *n. f.* a virgin.

Oꞁꞁꝺ, *n. m. pl.* sledges

Ól, *v.* (*imp. and inf.)*
drink.

Olꞁꞁnn, *n. f. dat.* in
wool.

Olann, *n. f.* wool.

Olc, *adj.* bad, wicked.

Ólfainn, *v.* (*cond.*) I would drink.

Óp, *n. m.* gold.

Opo, *n. m.* a sledge.

Opm, *pr. pron.* on me.

Oppaib, *pr. pron.* on you.

Óp, *prep.* over.

Oċpap, *n. m.* illness, distemper.

Páipoe, *n. m.* a child.

Páipoeaó, (*gen. pl.* of children.

Páopaic, *n. m.* Patrick

Peacaó, *n. m.* sin.

Peavaipi, *gen.* of Peter

Peavap, *n. m.* Peter.

Péin, *n. f. dat.* pain.

Péipc, *n. f.* a reptile.

Pian, *n. f.* pain.

Pigin, *n. f.* a penny.

Pigne, *n. f. pl.* pence.

Pobail, *n. f. gen.* of a people.

Pobal, *n. m.* a people.

Póg, *n. f.* a kiss.

Póg, *v.* (*imp.*) kiss.

Póg, *v.* (*past. indic.*) kissed

Popc, *n. m.* a fort.

Popcláipge, *n. f.* Waterford.

Póp, *v. imp.* marry.

Pópaó, *v.* (*inf.*) (to) marry.

Pópaó, *n. m.* marriage

Pópann, *v* (*hab.*) marries

Ppiom, *adj.* chief, first.

Ppoinn, *n. f.* a dinner a meal.

Pup, *n. m.* a lip.

Raċpaó, *v.* 1*st. pers. fut.* I will go.

Raóapc, *n. m.* sight.

Raib, *v.* (*subj.*) was (may be.)

Ráin, *n. f. dat.* a spade.

Rán, *n. f.* a spade.

Rann, *n. m.* a verse, a song.

Rannaió, *n. m.* a songster.

Rig, *n. m.* a king.

Riagail, *n. f.* a rule.

Ró, *intens. par.* very, too much.

Ro, *par.* with past tense.

Ró-beag, *adj.* too small

Ró-ṁóp, *adj.* exces- Saop, *n.m.* a carpenter,
sively great, too large. a builder.
Ró-ḟean, *adj.* very old. Saop, *adj.* free, cheap.
Ró-ċeiċ, *adj.* too hot. Saopóuine, *n. m.* a
Ruaó, *adj.* red. freeman.
Rún, *n. m.* a secret, a Saoċaip, *n. m. gen.* of
desire. work.
Saʒaipc, *n.m. gen.* and Saoċap, *n. m.* work,
pl. priests. labour.
Saʒapc, *n. m.* a priest. Sáp, *intens. par.* very,
Saióбip, *adj.* rich, fer- most.
tile. Sáp-binn, *adj.* most
Sail, *n. f.* a beam. harmonious.
Sa m-baile, *adv.* at Sáp-ʒlic, *adj.* very wise
home; *see* a m-baile. Sáp-ṁaiċ, *adj.* very
Saoʒail, *n. m. gen.* of good, excellent.
the world. Sápuʒaó, *n.m.* oppres-
Saoʒal, *n.m.* the world, sion, fatigue.
the age. Scáċ, *n. m.* a shadow.
Saoʒalaċ, *adj.* long Sciaċ, *n. f.* a shield.
lived. Scoil, *n. f.* a school.
Saoi, *n. m.* a sage. Scolaipe, *n. m. (nom.*
Saoil, *v. (imp.)* think, *and gen.)* a scholar.
suppose. Scpioḃ, *v. (imp.)* write.
Saoil, *v. (past. indic.)* Scpioḃ *(rel. past.)*(who)
thought. wrote.
Saoileann, *v. (hab.)* Scuip, *v. (imp.)* cease.
thinks. Sooc, *n. m.* a trumpet.
Saoip, *n. m. pl.* car- Sé, *pers. pron.* he, it.
penters. Sé, *num.* six.

Seaċáın, v. (imp.)shun, avoid.

Seaċnaú, v. (inf.) (to) avoid.

Seaċt, num. seven.

Seaċtoeuᵹ, num. seventeen.

Seaċtṁaú, num. seventh.

Seaċtṁaú-oeuᵹ, ord. num. seventeenth.

Seampóᵹ, n. f. a shamrock.

Sean, adj. old.

Sean-bean, n. f. an old woman.

Seanouıne, n. m. an old man, old person.

Seanƒeaⱷ, n.m. an old man.

Scaⱷc, n. m. and f. love.

Seaⱷ, v. (imp.) stand.

Ṡeaⱷ, v. (past indic.) stood.

Seaⱷṁaċ, adj. firm.

Séoeuᵹ, num. sixteen.

Séıo, v. (imp.) blow.

Ṡéıo, v. (past. indic.) blew.

Seınn, v. (imp.) sing.

Séıⱷe, n. m. a supper, a meal.

Seıⱷeaú, ord. num. sixth.

Seıⱷeaú-oeuᵹ, ord. num. sixteenth.

Seoo, n. m. a jewel.

Seoıl, n. m. gen. of a sail.

Seol, n. m. a sail.

Seunṁaⱷ, adj. prosperous.

Sᵹıan, n. f. a knife.

Sᵹⱷıoⱷ, v. (imp.) ravage, ruin.

Sí, pers. pron. she.

Sıao, pers. pron. they.

Sıao-ⱷın, pron. those.

Sıao-ⱷo, pron. these.

Sıb, pron. you, ye.

Sın, dem. pron. that.

Sınn, pers. pron. we.

Sıon, n. f. the weather, a blast.

Síoⱷ, adv. down.

Ṡíoⱷ, adv. below.

Sıúbaıl, v. (imp.) walk

Sıubal, v. (inf.) to walk

Ṡıúbalⱷaınn, v. (cond' I would walk.

Sıúⱷ, n. f. a sister.

Sláinte. *n. f. nom.* and *gen.* health.

Slait, *n. f. dat.* (to) a rod.

Slán,*adj.* healthy, safe

Slána, *adj.* (*pl.* of ɼlán) healthy.

Slat, *n.f.* a rod.

Smíʒeaḋ,*n.m.* a smile.

Smíʒeaḋa, *n. m. pl.* smiles.

Smioɼ, *n. m.* marrow.

Snátaḋ, *n.f.* a needle

So, *dem. pron.* this.

Só, *prefix,* implying ease, opposite to ḋó.

Sóḃeuɼaċ, *adj.* well-mannered.

Soċaɼ, *n. m.* profit.

So-ḋeunta, *part. adj.* possible.

Sóɼeicɼionaċ, *adj.* visible, easy to be seen.

Sóʒ, *n. m.* pleasure, ease, comfort.

Soiɼḃiʒ (*v.*), prosper.

Soiɼḃiʒiḋ, *v.(opt.)* may prosper.

Soluɼ, *n. m.* light.

Sona, *adj.* happy, fortunate.

Spailpín, *n. m.* a labourer.

Spaɼán, *n.m.* a purse.

Speal, *n.f.* a scythe.

Spáiḋ, *n. f.* a street.

Spɼian, *n. m.* a bridle.

Spóin, *n.f. dat.* a nose

Spón, *n.f.* a nose.

Sput, *n. m.* a stream.

Suan, *n.m.* rest, sleep.

Suaɼ, *adv.* up.

Suaɼ, *adv.* above.

Súḃáilce, *n.f.* virtue.

Suiḋe, *n. m.* (*nom.* and *gen.*) sitting, a session

Suiḋeaċán, *n.m.* a seat

Súil, *n. f.* an eye.

Súil,*n.f. gen. pl.* of eyes

Sul, *adv.* before.

Tá, *v.* (*pres. indic.*)am, is, are.

Tabaiɼ. *v.* (*imp.*) give.

Tabaiɼt, *v.* (*inf.*) (to) give, giving.

Taḋʒ,*n.m.* Teig, Thaddeus.

Taiḋʒ, *n. m. gen.* of Teig.

Táim,*v.* (*1st pres.*)I am

Tainic, *v.* (*past indic.* came.

Táir, v. (pres. indic. 2nd) thou art.

Tairbeac, adj. profitable.

Talam, n. f. the earth.

Tamaill, n. m. gen. of a while.

Tamall, n. m. a while.

Tangaoar, v. (past ind. 3rd) they came.

Tangar, v. (past indic. 1st) I came.

Tar, v. (imp.) come thou

Tar, prep. over, beyond

Tarb, n. m. a bull.

Tart, n. m. thirst.

Té, n. m. he, who, an individual, an té.

Teac, n. m. a house.

Teact, v. (inf.) (to) come, coming.

Teanga, n. f. a tongue, a language.

Teann, adj. tight.

Téió, v. (imp.) go.

Teine, n. f. fire.

Teit, adj. hot.

Tig, v. comes.

Tig (dat.), house.

Tige, n. m. gen. of a house

Tigearna, n. m. a lord.

Tinn, adj. sick.

Tiocfá, v. (cond. 2nd.) thou wouldst come.

Tiopma, adj. pl. of tirm, dry.

Tir, n. f. country, land.

Tir-gráó, n. m. patriotism, country-love.

Tirm, adj. dry.

Tobair, n. m. gen. of a well.

Tobar, n. m. a well.

Tóg, v. (imp.) take, lift

Toil, n. f. will.

Tomáir, n. m. gen. of Thomas.

Tomás, n. m. Thomas.

Tonn, n. m. and f. a wave.

Tor, Torac, n. m. a beginning.

Tre, prep. through.

Treas, prep. through.

Treas, ord. num. third.

Treas-oeug, thirteenth

Treun, adj. brave, strong.

Treunfear, n. m. a brave man

Τρí, *num.* three.

Τριαν, *n. m.* a third.

Τρí-ϭeuϫ, *num.* thirteen

Τρócαιρeαċ, *adj.* merciful.

Τρom, *adj.* heavy.

Τρoṁ-ṫuαn, *n. m.* a heavy sleep, a lethargy.

Τρuαϫ, *adj.* sad.

Τú, *pers. pron.* thou.

Τú.*pers.pron.*thee(acc.)

Τuαιριm. *n. f.* a guess, a hint.

Τuαm, *n. f.* Tuam.

Τuαmα, *n. f. gen.* of Tuam.

Τú ṗéιn, *pers. pron. emph.* thyself.

Τuϫ,*v.*(*past indic.*)gave

Τuιϫ, *v.* understand.

Τuιϫριn, *v.* (*inf.*) (to) understand.

Τúρ, *n. m.* a beginning.

Uα,*n.m.* a grandson, a descendant; see o.

Uαιρle, *adj. pl.* of uαραl, noble, *n, pl.* gentlemen, nobles.

Uαιρleαċτ, *n. f.* nobility.

Uαṁαn, *n. m.* fear, dread.

Uαραl, *adj.* noble.

Uαċϭáρ, *n. m.* terror.

Uϭ, *n. f.* an egg.

Uϭαll, *n. m.* an apple.

Uϭαllϫoρτ, *n. m.* an orchard.

Úϫϭαρ, *n. m.* an author

Uí, *n. m. gen.* of a descendant; *see* o and uα.

Uιϭe, *n. f. pl.* eggs.

Uí Ϭonnαϭáιn, *n. m. gen.* of O'Donovan.

Uιle, *adj. pron.* all.

Uιρϫe, *n. m.* (*nom. and gen.*) water.

Ull, *adj.* great.

Ullṗéιρτ, *n. f.* a monster, a great serpent

Um, *prep.* about.

Uṁlαċτ, *n. f.* humility.

Uρláιρ, *n.m. pl.* floors.

Uρláρ, *n. m.* a floor.

Uρρα, *n. f.* a prop, jamb.

CRÍOĊ.

www.ingramcontent.com/pod-product-compliance
Lightning Source LLC
Chambersburg PA
CBHW030545270326
41927CB00008B/1518